THE ADOLESCENT GAP

THE ADOLESCENT GAP

Research Findings on Drug Using and Non-Drug Using Teens

By

EDWARD M. SCOTT, Ph.D.

Clinic Director
Oregon Alcohol and Drug Treatment
and Training Center
Associate Clinical Professor of Psychiatry
University of Oregon Medical School
Portland, Oregon

Foreword by

Rev. Theodore M. Hesburgh, C.S.C.

President
University of Notre Dame
Notre Dame, Indiana

With a Chapter by

Chuck Paulus

Counselor
Oregon Alcohol and Drug Treatment
and Training Center
Portland, Oregon

CHARLES C THOMAS • PUBLISHER
Springfield • Illinois • U.S.A.

Published and Distributed Throughout the World by
CHARLES C THOMAS • PUBLISHER
Bannerstone House
301-327 East Lawrence Avenue, Springfield, Illinois, U.S.A
Natchez Plantation House
735 North Atlantic Boulevard, Fort Lauderdale, Florida, U.S.A.

© *1972, by* CHARLES C THOMAS • PUBLISHER

ISBN 0-398-02403-0

Library of Congress Catalog Card Number: 73-175084

With THOMAS BOOKS careful attention is given to all details of manufacturing and design. It is the Publisher's desire to present books that are satisfactory as to their physical qualities and artistic possibilities and appropriate for their particular use. THOMAS BOOKS will be true to those laws of quality that assure a good name and good will.

Printed in the United States of America
RN-10

This book is dedicated to

My wife, Kathy, whose mothering skills have, by blending wisdom, constancy, and freedom, avoided the adolescent gap with our children.

Our children, Kathleen, Michael, Maureen, Timothy, and Molly, who do not avoid putting their shoulder against the wind.

FOREWORD

Youth in today's society is both our greatest challenge and our greatest resource. Youth is a challenge in that the abrasions, frictions, and conflicts between the youth of today and the older generation have become more obvious, more stridently expressed, and more radical and significant than ever in the past. This clamor on the part of youth is discomforting and even confounding to many of the older generation precisely in that it is a direct confrontation with the commitments expressed in both our lives and our teachings. However, youth is our greatest resource because it will provide the future leaders of our society, and especially because in its outspoken fashion, it confronts what is weak or shoddy in our way of life. Young people today express a deep moral commitment. Youth speaks to us of peace, nonviolence, love, and an authentic humanism. In its idealism and commitment, youth offer the prospect of a future which is filled with hope more than at any time in the past.

Of all the facets of the so-called youth culture, the most disconcerting and alarming is the prevalence of the use of drugs. Aware as we are of the horrifying prospects associated with drug addiction and even drug abuse, it is difficult for older adults to take a dispassionate look at drug use among young people. The high association between drug use and crimes against person and property is alarming and seemingly inconsistent with the idealism prominent in the so-called youth culture. Thus there has developed a national concern with the problems associated with drug use. All too often the problem of drugs is linked with youth or with students. The use and abuse of drugs is a growing problem with all strata of our society. However, the focus of attention is often limited to young people.

The extent of this national concern is expressed in the programs, committees, and governmental agencies which have been established in our efforts to understand and control this problem. Hundreds of books and thousands of articles have been produced in the last few years which deal with this issue.

This is the context in which Dr. Scott's volume appears. However, in its way this book is refreshingly different and takes a different approach to the scientific research reports and the weighty essays by scholars addressed to other scholars. This book speaks to the person concerned with youth and who works with young people. It communicates an insight into young people without the complexities of ponderous theories or elaborate methodologies. It is direct and forceful in that the young people speak directly to us in their words. This provides a fuller and more human understanding of their thoughts, feelings, and motives.

Through this book, Dr. Scott has permitted young people to share their point of view. These young people include drug users, former drug users, and young people who have never used drugs. This provides a complete picture, the full range of motives for getting involved with drugs, and for giving them up. The rationale for the seemingly irrational activity of drug use becomes more clear. Counselors, teachers, parents, and adults who are concerned about young people will hopefully find some insights in these pages; this volume offers an understanding that will assist them in working with young people before they are likely to become involved in drug use, with young people who are in conflict about drugs, and even with young people who accept drug use as part of their way of life.

One message comes through very clearly in the words of the youth who speak to us here. This is the message of the title. Young people are not all alike. The resentment and frustration at being stereotyped and therefore not heard, not related to, not accepted as individual persons is very evident. Perhaps this message is even more important than the insights and information regarding drug use.

This is a very personal book. It contains facts and figures, but only to provide the context for young people to speak out in their own words. This book provides information, but much more it leads to understanding and compassion. Dr. Scott has long been identified with his efforts to work with young people and people of all ages in problems of drug and alcohol abuse. We are very grateful to him for sharing the significant insights he has achieved through his clinical work, and particularly for making it possible for youth to speak to us in their own words in this book. One can only hope that it will bear fruit in preserving and nurturing our greatest resource for the future, the young people of today.

(REV.) THEODORE M. HESBURGH, C.S.C.

PREFACE

I HAVE chosen one problem area confronting present-day teen-agers — drugs — as a focal point for this book. In an attempt to avoid remarks springing Zeus-like from my thoughts, teen-agers themselves, through countless, selfless hours, gave the main ideas.

Certainly, a book about teen-agers should flow from teen-agers. The teen-ager, as an emergent adult, does not fit neatly into a single conceptualized package, either with a blue ribbon or a pink ribbon. Facts, as fiction, are often slanted. However, some categories were developed to allow data and information to be collected in a meaningful manner. The three categories are

1. Non-drug using teen-agers.
2. Teen-agers who have stopped using drugs.
3. Teen-agers who have not stopped using drugs and state that they plan continual use of drugs.

This rounded version, I hope, more accurately reflects the whole scene — drugs, non-drugs, and therapeutic aspects, rather than funneled views of the abuser alone.

The therapeutic aspects should provide some solace for parents whose teen-ager is using drugs, as well as the teen-ager who wants out of the drug scene. There are real alternatives available other than drug abuse.

For the teen-ager who is using drugs and who plans to continue using drugs, ideas and materials are provided so he may obtain a clearer view of the price he elects to pay. He may also see ways out, should he so choose.

The data obtained from the teen-agers who use drugs and from those who do not use drugs suggest some sharp, clear, and precise differences, so much so that there is *an adolescent gap.*

Lastly, the discussion in the final chapter gives an overview of the findings, with an attempt to present an in-depth view of one of the major findings — experience.

ACKNOWLEDGMENTS

A BOOK such as this "grows out" of the participation of adolescents. I want to thank *all* of them who took part in the questionnaires, those who were patients in groups, as well as those adolescents who were members of discussion groups for a wide variety of audiences.

A critical reading of the manuscript and several notable suggestions were contributed by Hal Nevis, M.D. and Mike Giammatteo, Ph.D. Their help is gratefully acknowledged.

I want to give a special note of thanks to Rev. Hesburgh, President of the University of Notre Dame, for taking time from his busy schedule to read the manuscript and write a foreword.

Lastly, to Mrs. Judy Smith, who was able to interpret my handwriting and type and retype numerous portions of the draft, thanks.

Acknowledgment is given to Harper and Row, Publishers for permission to quote from *Zen Buddhism and Psychoanalysis*, by Fromm, Suzuki and deMartino.

E. M. S.

CONTENTS

THE ADOLESCENT GAP

Chapter I

OVERVIEW

THIS chapter will briefly concern itself with four issues: a) the rationale for the title of the book *Adolescent Gap* b) some literary references to drug use, c) delineation of the major drug classifications, and d) description of research methods.

DIFFERENCES BETWEEN DRUG ABUSING AND NON-DRUG-USING TEEN-AGERS

I have purposefully avoided the "thin-worn," meaningless phrase "generation gap" because in my opinion it is a cliche. By this, I mean, it is a "ready-made" solution by either saying too much or it says nothing. It is, in addition, a kind of "cop-out" and polarizes the source of the problem outside one's self or outside one's peer group. A psychological axiom, and an easy proclivity, is to always look for the source of one's problems within another group, or at least outside the self. The "bad guy" is always "out yonder, pardner." The "given" in psychological parlance is that I am the "good guy" and I belong to a "good bunch" — it is the other groups or organizations which cause the problem — "out thereism." I have yet to hear of an investigative committee, which has attempted to learn the "facts" in labor groups, in minority groups, in church groups, in the American Psychological Association, or the American Medical Association which blames itself for its major problems. Instead, a kind of "mirable dictu" (wonderful to say) is operative by stating the cause of the problems we are having rests on the shoulders of "outsiders" — "out thereism"!

Furthermore, reaction and tension between adults and the younger folk is nothing new.

In *Faust,* a student rants,

While half the world beneath our yoke is brought.
What have you doddards done? Nothing thought,

3

> dreamed, and considered drafting plan on plan!
> Age is an ague — fever it is clear, with chills
> of moody want and dread whoever's passed his
> thirtieth year is really just the same as dead.

(Note the reference to age thirty!)
Mephistopheles replies,

> Go on thy glorious way, eccentric youth!
> 'Twould grieve thee much, this truth to bear.
> No man can have a wise or foolish thought that
> in the past was not by others taught!

A partially recorded conversation with a teen-aged girl might prove an orienting note. A teen-age girl who had taken marijuana, followed by an averse reaction to mescaline, offers a form of orientation in terms of her evaluations at one of our therapy sessions.

Therapist: What about the generation gap?

Susie: Most kids and most parents are sick of hearing about it.

Therapist: What about the adolescent gap?

Susie: I've never heard of it.

Therapist: It means that there are differences among teen-agers.

Susie: If most parents realized that there is a big gap among kids, there wouldn't be such a big gap between parents and kids. Parents think every teen-ager takes drugs. Every magazine speaks of it.

Therapist: What about the teen-agers themselves?

Susie: Huge differences.

Therapist: Could you tell me something about the groupings?

Susie: Well, let's see — about 5 or 6 groups. First, there's the groups of popular kids. They haven't a group, but they stand out. They're outgoing, nice looking, and wear good clothes.

Therapist: Popular?

Susie: Ya, but more self-confident. I have some friends in that group. Second, is the real nice kids. They study, and get good grades. They don't go out much, are quiet. They like each other. Then, the third group, is the dumb ones, from grade school, and they hang around with each other. The fourth group are the drifters. They go from one group to another. I'm sort of that way, but not much any more. Fifth, I guess, is the hippies. They don't care how they dress. Some are nice, some aren't. Sixth, are the drug group. Some of these are in all the groups.

Therapist: How do these groups get along?

Susie: The hippies are always ranking other groups, calling them names. Hippies are hypocritical. They're supposed to be interested in big problems in the world, but often all they talk about is parties. They're just trying to get their own way. They go to the principal and try to make things their way, but it all comes down to just one thing — fighting the principal.

I feel relieved seeing you, Dr. Scott. Sometimes I change my opinions. What you said about kids' attitudes changing after they're on drugs was helpful. When I was smoking grass, I didn't think it was bad, if I wasn't caught. Kids' attitudes change often when on drugs. They all think the parents are against them. If parents care, the kids lie and get angry at their parents and tell more lies."

Support for the script just read is forthcoming from researchers as well as from youth.

Gould (1971) commenting on the hippie group writes,

> This is anything but a uniform group, because one sees among its members the most regressed of schizophrenics, who consume enormous quantities of pot and other drugs to conjure up another world, however unreal, because it seems better than the one they are living in.

Thomas (1971) lists the following groups of youth: a) the revolutionist, b) the new activist, c) the concerned liberal, d) the uncommitted, e) the common-man complacent, f) the concerned conservative, g) the reactionary activist, h) the reactionary supremist, i) the happener/swinger, j) the alienated hostile.

Thomas' categories includes both teen-agers and young adults (college youth).

The important point, and obviously I do feel it important, is that there is a wide variation (gap) among teen-agers themselves. Let's not "lump them," as we (as adults) do not want to be "lumped" by them. This point is illustrated by a police officer who asked a teen-ager, "Why do you call us pigs?" The teen-ager replied, "Why do you call us punks?"

In conversations with teen-agers, all agree that differences do exist among their peers, although all did not agree with "Susie's" classification. The important factor is that differences do exist among adolescents. Hence the title for this book: *The Adolescent Gap*.

Mary, a teen-aged girl who I had been seeing for drug abuse, in one of the psychotherapy sessions said, "I found that even my acquaintances were users, they treated me with indifference or outright dislike, and they hadn't before. This wasn't just what drugs made me think, it actually was! Everyone can take drugs, I take them but I don't like other people who do. I don't think this shows that they care for others. They don't like other people who destroy themselves, but what about them? Now that I have stopped I'm still the 'bummer.' People are *strange.*" Here is an "in-ward" gap — an adolescent gap within one person.

The experimented design could have revolved around a number of differences: delinquent versus nondelinquent; or middle class versus lower class adolescents, etc.

Due to the current interest in drug abuse among adolescents, I felt that a study which compared drug abusing versus non-drug using teen-agers would serve, hopefully, a timely, inquisitive interest among the lay public as well as in professional groups.

Additionally, a group of teen-agers who had stopped their drug abuse were included as a vista of hope — an avenue of help. By including this "reformed" group, we hope to offer a suggestion of direction that could grant hope to numerous parents, as well as by their teen-agers who are searching for help.

LITERARY REFERENCES TO DRUG ABUSE

Some literary references to drugs might prove interesting.
>Oh true Apothecary!
>Thy drugs are quick.

In Shakespeare's play *Romeo and Juliet,* Romeo contacted a druggist (in Shakespeare's time an apothecary) to end his life, since he could no longer endure his grief. Romeo approaches the apothecary and says,

> . . . let me have a dram of poison; such soon-speeding gear as will disperse itself through all my veins. That the life-weary taken may fall dead.

The apothecary replies, "Such mortal drugs I have; but

Mantua's law is death to any utters them. "

Romeo quickly dispels the apothecary's reluctance, appealing to his poverty; and, the apothecary directs Romeo,

> Put this in any liquid thing you will and drink it off; and, if you had the strength of twenty men, it would dispatch you straight.

Romeo pays in gold,

> . . . worse poison to man's soul . . .

He hurries, then to Juliet's grave where after a somewhat lengthy speech declares,

> Here's to my love! (drinks)
> Oh true apothecary!
> Thy drugs are quick
> Thus with a kiss I die. (dies)

Perhaps the speech is a bit flowery, but the manner of handling problems, with less drastic drugs, reveal similarities to our own time. Drugs have been one problem solving method appearing in literature from the past to tomorrow's headlines.

Mention is made of drugs in other literary works. For instance, in Homer's *Odyssey* reference is made to opium; and perhaps most readers are familiar with, *Confession of an English Opium Eater,* by De Quincey.

A recent novel by Fuller (1970) entitled *Flight,* depicts the conflicts drug usage brings not only to the user but to his family. *Flight* is a delightful novel, and can be read with benefit both by parents and teen-agers.

DRUG CLASSIFICATION

This portion of the overview is an attempt to give the reader a summary of drug classification, associated with a series of vital questions. Summaries of drug classifications by other authors can be consulted for a more definitive chemical, medical, and psychiatric delineation.

Hallucinogens

A. Facts

1. LSD (lysergic acid diethylamide) is a semi-synthetic derived

from the ergot fungus of rye — a substance that grows on grain. Other hallucinogens are the following:

   a. Mescaline: A chemical from the peyote cactus.
   b. Psilocybin: A compound isolated from a special type of Mexican mushroom better known as "the magic mushroom."
   c. DMT: A powerful drug, somewhat like LSD.

2. Slang names: Acid, cubes.
3. How taken: Orally (dropped) as tablets, but it can be disguised as a powder or liquid — even found on chewing gum, etc.
4. Sensory intensification and distorting are its most common effects. The mental or emotional aspects vary from anti-social behavior, to panic, to murder or to suicide.

Eveloff (1968) notes that the three most basic subjective responses to LSD are the following:

   a. Expectations.
   b. Loss of cohesiveness.
   c. Hypersuggestibility, that is, "With his reflexive modes of perception and cognition jarred loose, the user's judgment of the stimuli impinging upon him is impaired. What someone else says or what the subject thinks, be it frightening or pleasurable, can seem to be a perceptual and emotional reality."

5. Dilation of the pupils is one way to spot a user. Mood changes from laughing to crying and the appearance of being "lost in his thoughts" are often accompanied by taking of LSD.

B. Source of Danger

Precipitation of a psychotic episode — W. Frosch (1969) on the basis of his clinical work with users concludes, ". . . . it is a potentially dangerous drug when self-administered."

C. Why Used

In general, the user wants to "expand" his mind, arrive at insights, see things as they "are"; or to come to some type of personal, and world philosophy, maybe to increase his artistic ability.

Leary (1966) the "high priest" of LSD, wrote about two new commandments which were "revealed to me . . ." as the result of ". . . some 250 psychedelic sessions." Today, as we read about Leary's behavior, his words strike a macabre note.

D. *Historical Note*

LSD was first synthesized in 1938 by Hofman, in Switzerland. For a time it was felt that LSD could be used therapeutically as a "model psychosis," but the majority of authorities do not presently claim benefit from this.

E. *Controversy*

In general, authorities frown on the use of LSD. There is *at this time,* no definite proof that using LSD will cause chromosomal damage in humans, but there are some indications pointing in that direction.

F. *Clinical Case*

A portion of a letter written by an 18-year-old girl (Betty) will indicate some of the subjective experiences she underwent by using LSD.

> I dropped (my very first trip) Q-plus which is a derivative of LSD, but much stronger. About an hour later my body tingled clear through and I felt like I was glued to the couch. John suggested we go down to the basement so I could have a better trip. He had to literally pull me off the couch. It was all I could do to move or walk. The basement was pitch black. We sat on the steps and started rapping. The windows and walks started converging and pulling apart again. There was a stove directly in front of us and a snake-like red, bleeding dragon came out of it towards me. I shut my eyes, blinked a couple of times, and the hallucination disappeared. I knew they were hallucinations at the time, but my baser instincts reacted normally as if it were very real, and I wondered a couple of times if they were or not. I don't remember all the things I saw, but they were basically the same. When John looked at me once, his face had transformed into a

hideous monster; long, bushy, matted hair dripping with blood, his eyes were wild, bloodshot, and sort of luminous. He had a terribly wicked smile. I must admit I screamed for all I was worth! We went back up the stairs and about the third step from the top, a pair of white hands appeared and grabbed for my ankles. I jumped and almost fell down the stairs, but John caught me.

G. Implication

By and large the "word" is around among young people that LSD is a dangerous drug and the amount used is tapering off.

Smart and Jones (1970), in comparing 100 LSD users with non-users, found "... a much higher incidence of psycho-pathology among LSD users than non-users; with conduct disturb-ance and psychosis being the most frequent diagnosis."

Amphetamines

A. Facts

1. Best known: Dexedrine®, Methedrine®, and Benzedrine®
2. Slang names: speed, dexies, and crystal.
3. Users are spotted by their restlessness, dilated pupils, dry mouth, and talkativeness.
4. Stimulants release norepinephrine, a substance stored in the nerve endings, to the higher center of the brain.

B. Source of Danger

Teen-agers themselves have formulated slogan, "Speed kills," referring to Methedrine, yet they do not heed their own warning. Heavy doses may cause a temporary psychosis, accompanied by hallucinations; and abrupt withdrawal may result in depression and suicide.

C. Why Used

Amphetamines are used to handle fatigue, which truck drivers commonly experience, or students at exam times. These kinds of drugs also produce feelings of alertness, self-confidence, and well being. They are also used to curb appetites in overweight individuals.

D. Historical Notes

Amphetamines were first produced in the 1920's. Originally these drugs were used medically as stimulants to the central nervous system. Recently studies show that young people are the greatest abusers of amphetamines, using them "for kicks" or "speeding."

E. Controversy

Most agree that unsupervised use of amphetamines is dangerous; intellectual and emotional breakdowns follow long usage.

F. Clinical Case

A 17-year-old boy tells the following:

> . . . grass, I took it only twice, then, I went to acid. . . Finally, in Frisco where I had a lot of friends and there I got taking speed and that was it, for a while. All I took was speed, it made me feel good. My head was light and I had a lot of energy. I took speed for about a month and then I stopped that and went back to acid and I realized what was happening wasn't enough. After taking speed again for a couple of weeks, when I came down from speed, I hated everything. I wanted to destroy everything. Whatever got in my way. I don't know how suicide got into the picture, but it did. Instead of seeing good things, I sensed everything that was evil. (Like what?) Like you say "hi" to your neighbor and he just walks away, or that everyone tries to outdo everyone.

It was at this point that his father phoned me, extremely concerned about his son's depression, anger, and suicidal thoughts.

G. Amphetamines and Other Drugs

Many users "combine" (alternate) the uppers (amphetamines) and the downers (barbiturates).

H. Implications

An investigation in San Francisco concluded that there were about 4,000 intravenous amphetamine users in that city. Garodetzky (1970) states, "It now appears that intravenous use of amphetamines, mostly involving methamphetamines, is becoming a dangerous and major drug abuse problem."

Tranquilizers and Sedatives

A. *Facts*

1. Sedatives are designed to relieve tension. There are 1,500 types available, but the most common types are Equanil®, Valium®, Librium®, Doriden®, and barbiturates.
2. Slang names: Sleepers, barbs, red-binds, yellow-jackets, etc.
3. The individual becomes sleepy, displays slurred speech, and, at times, falls into a coma.

B. *Source of Danger*

There are several dangers. Physical addiction is one of the most fearful prospects. Forgetfulness, accidental suicide, and psychotic behavior due to sudden withdrawal are other common dangers.

C. *Why Used*

Barbiturates enable the user to be relaxed, to be good natured, and to be social.

D. *Historical Note*

In 1863, barbituric acid was first synthesized; the first active derivative (barbital) as a depressant action was reported in 1902. The most common types are Nembutal®, Seconal®, and Amytal®.

E. *Controversy*

No controversy exists. These drugs are dangerous and must be used under *careful* medical supervision.

F. *Clinical Case*

One 17-year-old girl had a history of an intensive, 5-month use of marijuana and "5 hits of heroin which I didn't like; a three-month use of speed which tired me out, so I changed to barbiturates, which were cheaper and more relaxing."

Family problems became strained, and she took an overdose of Seconal and slashed her wrists. She was hospitalized (she was unconscious for 48 hours), returned home upon release from the hospital, and immediately began her use of barbiturates, ran away from home and "took reds to show that my parents couldn't hold me captive."

After she was apprehended, she was referred to the clinic.

Later in the book, Chapter III (p. 44), mention of wrist cutting and drug use by young females will be mentioned.

G. Other Drugs and Barbiturates

A most dangerous combination of drugs is alcohol and barbiturates; coma and death may result. As previously mentioned, youngsters often use a combination of "uppers" and "downers."

H. Implication

Directions for prescriptions must be carefully given by physicians and scrupulously adhered to by patients.

"Hard" Narcotics

A. Facts

1. Opium.
2. Morphine (from opium).
3. Heroin (from morphine).
4. Codeine (from opium).
5. Paregoric (contains opium).

B. Source of Danger

Addiction is almost certain.

C. Why Used

To "get away from it all." It is a "sleeper" drug, one of the most potent; no worries or problems "get" to the user, except the anxiety of securing the next fix.

D. Historical Note

Perhaps opium is the most ancient of all the drugs, since it is mentioned in Egyptian writing (medical tablets) in 16th century BC. Other ancient societies used opium to relieve pain and illness, and in a few countries it was a social "must" somewhat akin to alcohol in the United States. In the early 1800's the active ingredient in opium was isolated and given the name morphine (from Morpheus, who was supposed to be the god of dreams).

In the middle 1850's (with the invention of the hypodermic needle) the Civil War brought many injuries to soldiers and morphine was used to relieve pain. Addiction rather quickly followed; in fact, it was termed the "Army disease."

At the turn of the century (1900) heroin was derived from morphine. It was originally welcomed by the medical profession as a countermeasure to morphine addiction. Opium smokers soon learned that a little heroin, "did more" than many pipes of opium.

E. Controversy

No reputable individual, authority or lay, advocates the use of opium or its derivatives (except for short-term medical purposes).

There is, however, a controversy about methadone, which is the drug given to counteract addiction to hard narcotics.

F. Clinical Case

In therapy sessions (one year duration) a 20-year-old female now taking methadone (for the past six months) reported,

> I crave the scene again, not so much the drug as the scene. I find myself driving down to Williams Avenue. (Could you explain this action?) I don't crave the drug, Oh, I do, but then I know if I fixed I'd feel nothing, so I say to hell with it. But the scene, being caught

up in the pace, its excitement, never knowing what's going to happen next. Always action! If I look at it rationally, I don't like the fast pace, I hate it, yet I love it! That's schizophrenic! I hate to hurry and the paranoia, but it's the fastness. It's like New York, the bright lights. I like the dirtiness! (What?) It is an unclean life, in the gutter, and yet I'm attracted to it!

G. Implications

The treatment for hard narcotics is difficult. Methadone is a first, though crude step; in time, refinements may be discovered.

Marijuana

A. Facts

1. Marijuana is the dried top of the hemp plant.
2. Most often it is smoked from hand rolled cigarettes (a joint); a few individuals mix it with something and chew it.
3. Slang names: Pot, grass, weed, joint, and reefers.
4. Typical psychological effects: Marijuana produces in the user a sense of euphoria, hilarity, and well being; although some users become "glassy-eyed," stare off into space, or drift off into sleep.
5. Typical physical effects: Bloodshot eyes (red eye), dryness of mouth, increased pulse rate.

B. Source of Danger

What is dangerous about marijuana? At the present, we really are not certain, although it is known that one of the active elements in marijuana is due to the tetrahydrocannobinals (THC's), and as the dose of THC is increased, sensory distortions may appear.

Hollister (1971) in his efforts to summarize the latest findings on marijuana wrote, "As more reports come in, it appears that the immediate dangers are almost identical with those of LSD, probably because at higher doses many of the same mental and emotional reactions are obtained. What is more disturbing are the reports of subtle effects on the personality associated with prolonged use; loss of a desire to work, loss of motivation, loss of judgment and intellectual functions. It may well be argued that individuals with these manifestations may have developed them in the absence of drug use, but available evidence does not follow this assertion."

C. Why Used

There are several authors who attempt to explain the reactions most often associated with smoking marijuana. One of the better explanations which I have come across is by an anonymous author, in a chapter entitled, "Effects of Marijuana on Consciousness," appearing in a book edited by Tart (1969). The reader who wants to learn about this in depth should secure that chapter. In brief, an experience is either "pure" (no associations) or it is conscious (the experience is connected to meanings, plan, etc.). Marijuana assists the user to "get into" (to be part of, to exist in) what he is experiencing. This is its subtle but real "pull."

D. Historical Note

Marijuana is an ancient drug. It is known that in 3000 BC Emperor Shen Hung mentioned it in one of his writings; and marijuana was prescribed for many illnesses. Gradually, the use of marijuana spread to India where it was known as the "delight giver." But at other times, for example, in the eleventh century AD, during the conflict of Christians and non-Christians, one native leader, Hasan-l-Sabbah urged his warriors to consume large amounts of marijuana (hashish) in order to arouse his warriors into a state of anger and frenzy. Gradually, from local usage (in Arabic "hashisn"), the word "hashish" developed into the English word "assassin."

Here, then, is clearly indicated the sharp differences for which marijuana can be used: from "delight giver" to "assassin."

Eventually in 1913 marijuana made its way to the United States from Mexico, through the border towns of San Diego, California and El Paso, Texas. Incidentally the popular Mexican song "La

Cucaracha" concerns itself about a cockroach who could not work because it had no marijuana to smoke.

Attempts to estimate the use of marijuana in this country vary greatly; figures range from 3-12 million. These figures depend on the source of information.

E. *Controversy*

Marijuana! This is an excellent source from which to start an argument! People are either against marijuana (that it leads to other drugs) or are for it, "It is no worse than alcohol and only a small percentage of marijuana users go on to other drug use."

Although each side proclaim the latest evidence in its favor and, therefore, against the opposition, it seems to me that the "handling" (acceptance or rejection) of the data is more an emotional basis.

My position is that of being against marijuana. The American Medical Association's Committee on Alcoholism and Drug Dependence on Marijuana, appearing in the Journal of the American Medical Association states,

> Persons who use marihuana continually and as the symptomatic expression of a psychological conflict, a means of gaining social acceptance, or a way of escaping painful experience of anxiety or depression may be said to be psychologically dependent on the substance. Continuous use may be associated with the development of psychiatric illness, although few chronic users are admitted to psychiatric facilities. Chronic marihuana users often are lethargic, neglect their personal appearance, and occasionally may experience a deep sense of failure after believing they are capable of accomplishing great things.

F. *Clinical Case*

In one of his therapy sessions, John (a 17-year-old teen-ager) stated he hated his parents when he is smoking marijuana:

John: I still value them, it's just got to do with, they think what I'm doing is wrong.

Therapist: Do you forget the good times?

John: It does close you off, it detaches you. It, I don't know, when on grass, often the first two drags, I start to study each little action I make. Sometimes I use it when I listen to the stereo. I smoke pot by myself, that is when it is best. I haven't smoked with friends for a long time. I just enjoy the music, it heightens my hearing. I get more enjoyment. I get more enjoyment if I limit myself, say once a day. If I smoke it all the time, there's no difference.

Therapist: What about your grades?

John: I forget about 'em. After a period of time, it throws you off; that comes from wanting to smoke more grass. If I don't smoke for 1-2 weeks, I'm still thinking of it. After I come down, it doesn't seem real, so I want to do it again. My mind can't seem to record it.

Therapist: Preoccupied?

John: Ya, a whole little world drawn around it, and this world becomes more important. A lot of times I didn't know which world I was in, like I was out of my body — weird! Just on grass! a lot of it is subconscious. I just go blank and it is like I am asleep. People would be talking and I wouldn't be aware. A half ounce and I'm wiped out. I don't like that!

Therapist: Did you dream?

John: I'd dream during the day so I didn't have to dream at night. I'd be paralyzed in bed, crying and then sleeping and I'd get a feeling of fading. I'd open my eyes, I'd think I was asleep. I couldn't move out of bed, and I'd feel like I was getting sucked out of my bed. I'd get afraid.

G. Implication

The problem of marijuana is more involved than the mere legalizations of its use.

As the reports mount, there appears to be growing evidence that it is a potentially harmful drug.

Alcohol

A. Facts

1. Used, occasionally, by the majority of adults. Surveys among high school students indicate that usage varies from

localities; 8 out of 10 teens use alcohol in one locality compared with 2 out of 10 in another locality.
   a. The rate of alcoholism varies among the states; California is said to rank first.
   b. Urban areas have a higher rate of alcoholism than rural areas; San Francisco ranks first.
2. Slang names: Booze, juice, sauce.
3. The individual who has drunk too much can be easily spotted because of slurred speech, alcohol breath, and staggering gait.

B. *Source of Danger*

1. Psychological dependence.
2. Slow developing; on the average it takes 14 years to become an alcoholic.
3. About 7 million American are alcoholics.
4. Disruption of family life, drunken driving, loss of work.
5. Physical complications: Avitaminosis, cirrhosis, etc.

C. *Why Used*

1. Social lubricant.
2. Imitation of others.
3. Easily available.
4. Often a custom at gatherings.

D. *Historical Note*

Fermented and brewed beverages have been inbibed at least since 8,000 BC. The worshippers of alcohol enshrined alcohol as a god. Bacchus was the Greek god of wine, and every spring a quasi-religious, but certainly drunken orgy was held.

E. *Controversy*

By itself, alcohol has considerable adherents:
1. Some medical authorities feel that a little wine, even for patients, is helpful.

2. Others see alcohol as a "devil" leading its users astray.

F. Clinical Case

Susie, let's call her, is a 17-year-old high school student. During one of her therapy sessions she related, "I've been sad and depressed all the time."

Therapist: All the time?

Susie: Nothing makes me happy, I never enjoy *this* day. I'm always looking forward to something. I'm never happy with myself. Yesterday I got drunk, drank a case of beer.

Therapist: Let's hear more.

Susie: Three of my girl friends and I, last night, got some beer and drank it. We got it and drank it out in the woods, went and had a hamburger, then went to Betty's house and drank her father's liquor and then we danced. Last night was prom night. Proms aren't what they used to be. Ten years ago proms were important, you *had* to go.

Therapist: Last night you drank?

Susie: We drink often, every week end, well, to party. I don't like the taste. I like to get drunk and to get relaxed, its a great feeling.

Therapist: A great feeling?

Susie: I get all numb, and, no, high.

Therapist: Let's see, you get relaxed, numb and high? Could you tell me more about this?

Susie: I feel relaxed. I don't care what I say. When I'm numb, my hands and my face, like novocaine, from the dentist, it hits me later. I don't plan on it. High! High, I feel like I want sex, a boy friend, and make out.

Therapist: Have you used drugs?

Susie: Four or five times, a joint, maybe. I'm scared of any of the hallucinogins. I'd never use them.

Therapist: "What about grass?"

Susie: "I'd rather get drunk. I'm more sure of it."

Therapist: "Sure of it?"

Susie: "I know what's going to happen. I've been drunk so

many times, 50 or more times. I look forward to it. It's *fun to be drunk.*"

G. *Implications*

Alcohol is neither as dangerous as its opponents insist, nor as harmless as its adherents claim.

Longitudinal studies, for instance by Jones (1968), indicate that certain personality charactcristics predate, at least to some degree, drinking patterns during the high school years. Among these are the following:

1. Assertive.
2. Rebellious.
3. Pushing the limits.
4. Overtly hostile.

I have written at length about alcoholism, and presented a therapy program for teen-aged problem drinkers (Scott, 1970).

DESCRIPTION OF RESEARCH DESIGN AND RESEARCH SUBJECTS

Several methods of research came to my mind. After careful consideration, I felt a questionnaire would be the most appropriate method of data gathering.

Sherif and Sherif (1965) argue that any research method is inappropriate ". . . before rapport is firmly established."

In the present instance, care was taken to establish rapport.

The population (345 subjects) of the present study can be described as urban (Portland, Oregon metropolitan area), white, middle class students, attending public high schools. This study does not include lower class, minority groups, or teen-agers in mental institutions.

During one of the class periods, the teacher explained to the class the research project, concerned with the use or non-use of drugs.

The design called for student selection of the questionnaires they would complete. To accomplish this, the teacher indicated that on the desk in front of the room, there were three groups of questionnaries.

1. One group of papers were questions for teen-agers who had

not used drugs.

2. The second group of papers, was for those teen-agers who had used drugs and were still continuing to use them.

3. Another group of papers contained questions for teen-agers who had used drugs at one time but had stopped using them.

The groups of questionnaries were carefully indicated, so willing students could select the appropriate questionnaire. All students were asked to participate, but no pressure to participate was executed. Students were told not to put their names on the questionnaires, so they could feel free to answer the questions honestly and frankly without fear of identification. Additionally, the teacher assured the students that he was not interested in watching to see what group of questionnaires was selected.

No attempt was made to assess the number of students answering the questionnaires, and, therefore, the following figures do not reflect percentages. It merely indicates the number of teen-agers who freely elected to participate in this research study.

The three categories sampled are as follows:

Category 1. Teen-agers who have not used drugs: 120 girls and 60 boys.

Category 2. Teen-agers who are using drugs: 55 girls and 25 boys.

Category 3. Teen-agers who have used drugs and stopped: 50 girls and 35 boys.

Chapter II

RESEARCH RESULTS WITH
NON-DRUG USING TEEN-AGERS

THIS chapter reflects the data obtained from administering a questionnaire (see Chap. I) to 180 teen-agers (120 girls and 60 boys) attending school in the Portland metropolitan area.

The respondents were free to reject or to accept the questionnaire. I did not make an effort to tabulate the percentage of those rejecting versus those accepting. My general impression is that most of the students accepted a questionnaire.

I had contacted the teachers earlier concerning my research; they explained the purpose of the questionnaires and research design to their students.

All students were given instructions to be frank, honest, and accurate. Since names were not requested, their anonymity was assured and hence they could feel free to answer how they felt.

Results of the self-selected questionnaires from 180 teen-agers who have not used drugs appear below. ("Not used drugs" refers to the use of illegal drugs, or drugs medically prescribed, but misused.)

Question I: In your own estimation, what is the *principle* reason you have not started to use drugs?

Content	Generic-Category	Boys	Girls	Percentage*
1. No need for drugs	Rationale/Respect	20	37	32%
2. Fear of drugs	Fear	7	31	21%
3. Education (taught in school)	Education	2	15	10%
4. Seen what it has done to others	Modeling	5	19	13%
5. Desire to face problems	Rationale/Respect	16	6	12%

---

*The percentage figures in this table as in all others, are "rounded off" and do not always indicate the exact figure.

6.	It is illegal	Fear	7	2	05%
7.	Religious reasons	Rationale/Respect	1	3	02%
8.	Wish of parents	Rationale/Respect	1	5	03%
9.	Friends do not	Modeling	1	2	02%
	Total		60	120	

Verbatim replies to the above questions are as follows:

1. A 17-year-old teen-age girl wrote, "Because I have an older brother and younger sister who are drug users. It has really messed up their brain. My brother has been in and out of jail because of drugs. He was paid to go to college but loused it up. They're just a mess. I don't want to see myself go that way."

2. A 16-year-old girl replied, "I haven't any reason to, I have taken the drug courses and feel I know many of the dangers involved. I also feel my life is ahead of me and I don't want to ruin it. Like a lot of kids, I have a lot of problems with my family and friends, but I don't feel drugs are the answer."

3. A 17-year-old teen-age boy stated, "I'm an athlete and I don't need a crutch. I've seen friends fall apart when using drugs."

4. Another 17-year-old boy reflected, "It seems stupid to me. Using drugs is only an escape and temporary at that. People who use them are just copping out on their jobs and responsibility. They cannot hack it, so they try to run off and hide; in so doing they bring more responsibility on others."

In attempting to handle the data I have considered a variety of groupings, finally arriving, I hope, not too arbitrarily, at the following:

GENERIC HEADING: RATIONALE/SELF-RESPECT

		Boys	*Girls*
1.	Fear	7	31
2.	Example of others (Modeling)	5	19
3.	Education	2	15
	Total	14	65

It can be seen that over half of the girls (65 out of 120, or 54%) have not tried drugs because of rationale/self-respect. Boys do not respond to such a degree since only 23 per cent claim not to use drugs of this "preventive avenue."

Obviously, I have employed the term rationale/self-respect in a broad, generic sense. I do not want to proceed in a sematic flurry of a logistic nature, but it does appear to me that rationale (reason) and self-respect can serve as a generic heading.

From the obtained data, it can be seen that fear is a factor of prevention. In many educated circles today (teachers, physicians, psychiatrists, psychologists, and social workers) this preventive element (rationale or reason) has been scorned. Yet this same group utilizes fear as a preventive avenue: "Buckle-up" before driving in the car, and reports are often given regarding the results of those who "buckle-up" and those who do not.

Fear is not, however, a preventive factor with some individuals, in fact, it is seductive. I think it was Schneidman who coined the term "psyche-gamblers," the Russian roulets, American style, who actively search for new ways to threaten their own lives.

Some of the sampled population chose as a preventive element, what I've termed "modeling" of the drug user. Several pertinent quotes from the teens emerge from the data. The former quote of a 17-year-old girl, "They're (my brother and sister) just a mess. I don't want to see myself that way."

So we see that "modeling" the ill effects of drug abuse is a powerful preventive factor for some. On the contrary, others "catch it"; later I will offer possible reasons for this difference.

Education measures have been selected as the principle reason for not using drugs by 15 of the 120 girls, or a percentage of 13 per cent of the girls.

Many individuals will say that such a percentage is not effective. This all depends on how we interpret "effective." If our demands are too high, very little in life is "effective," from marriage to criminal justice, to medical practice, to education in general. If we allow the term "effective" to indicate that a reasonable percentage of individuals are helped, then education is "effective" as a preventive measure against drug usage. The argument could become both useless and endless if a fixed percentage is rigidly demanded, not only in the present instance, but in numerous other instances.

The Self (Personal or Psychological)

This category is intended to refer to personal reasons for not using drugs. Said a bit differently, I mean to convey that this group of individuals chose not to use drugs for reasons other than fear, friends, law, etc. Their reason for not using drugs was more internal than external, and as such, could be termed rationale/self-respect.

RATIONALE/SELF-RESPECT

	Boys	Girls
1. No need for drugs	20	37
2. Want to face problems	16	6
Total	36	43

This category, according to the boys, is the most potent preventive factor; 60 per cent of the boys selected this type of preventive element, whereas 35 per cent of the girls referred to it as a preventive element.

We must now make an attempt to handle the data. The first notion which comes to my mind is that of masculinity. The boys want to face life squarely, or express a "do it themselves" type of attitude. Crutches, aids, drugs, and the like are felt to be a concession, which they prefer not to make.

Secondly, the boys might be saying, some allude to it secondarily, that the modeling of the drug-using adolescent male were not examples of masculinity. Recall the previous quote, "I'm an athlete and I don't need a crutch. I've seen friends fall apart when using drugs."

From the two above categories and self (or intrapersonal), we learn some significant factors which have assisted the respondents of this research in resisting the use of drugs.

I hope that these "leads," will be followed, expanded, amplified, and made effective in community programs and school settings for the prevention of drug usage.

The remainder of reasons given for not using drugs by the teen-aged respondents are suggestive of preventive factors and really no avenue of assistance should be ignored. For instance, "wish of parents" and "religious reasons," were effective in a small number of girl respondents (6%); whereas the fact that drugs are illegal has served as a preventive force in 11% of the boys.

Question II. What do you think would cause you to start taking drugs?

		Boys	*Girls*	*Percentage*
1.	Nothing (wouldn't regardless, etc.)	19	42	34%
2.	Friend's influence	3	12	08%
3.	Curiosity	3	12	08%
4.	Depressed (severely)	3	9	07%
5.	Emotional problems	8	3	07%
6.	Tragic event	5	5	05%
7.	Numerous problems	3	3	03%
8.	Boredom	3	2	03%
9.	Problems with family (rejected, divorced parents, etc.)	5	12	09%
10.	Poor grades	3	0	02%
11.	Forced	0	7	04%
12.	If legal	2	3	03%
13.	Getting drunk and not knowing	0	3	02%
14.	Tricked into it	3	3	03%
15.	Break up of romance	0	4	02%
	Total	60	120	

Verbatim replies to the above question are as follows:
1. "Most likely, great emotional strain," replied a 16-year-old boy.
2. An 18-year-old teen-age boy stated, "I don't think I would

ever start taking drugs."
3. "Nothing! How about that for a closed mind," replied an 18-year-old girl.
4. A 16-year-old girl stated, "If I were depressed and in a very bad mood, I might think about taking drugs."

From the previous question, we learned that 180 teen-agers presented reasons for not using drugs. It is safe to assume that these reasons might change, depending on a number of circumstances, either external or internal. Question II is an attempt to ascertain the magnitude of the dimension which might occur.

Once again I will try to categorize the data into more generic concepts, trusting this is a meaningful and helpful aid in understanding the data.

GENERIC HEADING: NOTHING

	Boys	Girls
1. Nothing (I just won't, etc.)	19	42

We learn from the respondents that regardless of change of circumstances, or whatever, the above percentage will not resort to the use of drugs.

We, of course, are not certain if these young people's resolve is *that* firm. Regardless, this finding does point up what I consider to be important: some young people just simply are not going to resort to taking drugs. Anticipating some of the other data, we will see that in all three categories "nothing" emerged as a response to start taking drugs, stopping and restarting of drug usage.

GENERIC HEADING: OTHERS (INTERPERSONAL REASONS)

	Boys	Girls
1. Friend's influence	3	13
2. Family problems	5	12
3. Break up of romance	0	4
Total	8	28

The obtained data reflects keenly that teen-age girls consider their emotional well-being dependent on others, and also, they appear to be more easily influenced than boys.

Family disturbance appears to be more of an upsetting element in a girl's life than in a boy's life. The teen-age girl can be more easily influenced to take drugs than teen-age boys. Hence, the cliche, "drugs are people substitutes," applies more to girls than to boys.

GENERIC HEADING: THE SELF (INTRAPERSONAL)

		Boys	*Girls*
1.	Curiosity	3	12
2.	Emotional problems	8	3
3.	Boredom	3	2
4.	Numerous problems	3	3
5.	Poor grades	3	0
6.	Depressed	3	9
7.	Tragic events	5	5
	Total	28	34

This group of respondents select personal reasons as a possible influence for future drug use. Since boys do not rely on others, but rely more on the self, it is understandable that they would select personal reasons.

Some of the sub-categories are of interest:
1. Curiosity is selected more frequently by the girls than the boys.
2. Girls feel depression could be a possible future reason for drug use.
3. Boys select emotional problems more frequently than girls.

As girls look at themselves and consider some of the possibilities which might trigger the use of drugs, "depression" and "problems" appear as possible motivating reasons. Whereas the boys leave out the choice of "emotional" which perhaps is somewhat accurately interpreted as inner-turmoil or conflict, most likely in relation to a goal or to some kind of achievement.

In another research, *An Arena For Happiness* (1971), it was learned that opinions of the source of happiness differed between boys and girls. For a delineation and clarification of the material, the above mentioned work is recommended.

Other reasons: Into this "catch-all" fall various possible reasons for future drug use — forced, tricked, legal, etc.

The present results can be a potential source for preventive programs, pointing up that changes in one's life, whether internal or external, could lead to the use of drugs as a release. Alternate means of handling pressures should be quickly proposed before the teen-ager selects drugs as a solution.

Question III. If you did start, what do you think would most help you to stop taking drugs?

		Boys	*Girls*	*Percentage*
1.	Help of parents	4	14	10%
2.	Therapist and/or clinic	17	20	20%
3.	Help of someone, real interest (*not* on drugs) like a friend	8	30	21%
4.	Myself (will power, insight)	6	16	18%
5.	Don't know what would help	8	12	11%
6.	Wouldn't start, so can't answer	2	6	04%
7.	Religion	4	8	07%
8.	Locked up (in jail or mental institution)	1	6	04%
9.	Associated with others trying to get off drugs	2	3	03%
10.	Bad scare associated with drugs	4	0	02%
11.	Miscellaneous	4	5	04%
	Total	60	120	

Verbatim replies to the above question are as follows:

1. "Solving the problem that got me started," was the answer of a 16-year-old girl.
2. Another 16-year-old girl replied, "I think I would need a lot of understanding from my parents; I would have to be accepted as a person, not an addict."
3. A 17-year-old boy wrote, "A really bad scare on drugs."
4. "If I started, I probably wouldn't want to get off them, unless they were addicting and then it is impossible to predict," was the reply of a 17-year-old male respondent.

This question is a "natural" consequence of the former one, granting that these respondents might start to use drugs, what would they choose as a source of help to get off drugs.

Once again, I will utilize generic headings in handling the data:

GENERIC HEADING: OTHERS (INTERPERSONAL HELP)

		Boys	*Girls*
1.	Friend (*not* on drugs)	8	30
2.	Others trying to stop taking drugs	2	3
3.	Therapist (or clinic)	17	20
4.	Parents	4	14
	Total	31	67

The data indicated that 55 per cent of the girls and 50 per cent of the boys felt that if they started to take drugs, *others,* as noted above, would be a most helpful influence to stop taking drugs.

The major sub-category of *help from others* is that of a *professional therapist and/or clinic,* especially chosen by the boys. It is tempting to interpret this finding that boys are more realistic than girls but such an intervention is premature. Girls choose a friend *not* taking drugs as most helpful.

From this data, we learn that "selection" of one's therapist is an important factor. Girls prefer other girls *not* on drugs; boys tend to prefer a professional therapist.

More of the girl respondents than the boy respondents felt

parents would be helpful. The lack of credence in others taking drugs is surprising. Yet, in view of the respondents' answers to Question I (recall "modeling") the present data might reflect an antipathy toward the peer drug abuser.

Uncertain: Thirteen per cent of the girls and 11 per cent of the boys placed themselves within this category. This is a rather sizable amount and the inability of knowing where to turn might hinder their recovery. Propaganda, of an educational sort, might be useful in suggesting sources of help to youthful drug abusers, in order to avoid uncertainty of where to turn for help.

The self (Intrapersonal)	*Boys*	*Girls*
1. Will power	6	16
2. Bad scare	4	0
Total	10	16

This entry could be entitled, *self help.* It is surprising that girls selected *will power* more often than boys. In Question I, the boys wanted to stand on their own feet, so to speak, but when in trouble, they do not rely on themselves as often as girls. This is puzzling. Is it a universally valid finding? I do not know.

Incidentally, it should be noted that *will power* is "creeping" back in to the professional literature. A recent book by Rollo May, *Love and Will* (1969) gives a prominent part to *will power.* May's utilization of this concept was prompted by his readings of Farber's *The Ways of the Will* (1968).

Briefly, Farber states that there are two kinds or orders of will, a *general* kind and a *particular* one. More important, in my estimation, is that Farber points out clearly that will power needs imagination on which to work. In other words, when one is lacking imagination, one is lacking will power. An attempt to tie this conceptual notion together with other concepts will be made in the last chapter.

Religion: It is my opinion that professional people often ignore, play down, and in a few instances, make light of religion as a source of help for any kind of emotional or behavioral problem. Yet, I could present a number of instances in which young people instantly stopped using drugs, due to a religious conversion or experience, and have maintained the "conversion."

Question IV — What is your best guess of why other young people use drugs?

	Boys	Girls	Percentage
1. Experience (fun, pleasure, high, etc.)	15	35	28%
2. Escape (from reality, their problems, etc.)	20	31	28%
3. Nothing good (only trouble, bummer, etc.)	6	6	07%
4. Belonging to a group	2	20	12%
5. Trying to find themselves	0	8	04%
6. Curious	2	2	02%
7. Get back at parents	3	3	03%
8. To be different	6	4	05%
9. Cannot understand it	4	9	07%
10. Miscellaneous	2	2	02%
Total	60	120	

Verbatim examples to the above questions are as follows:

1. "Release from pressures in their environment," is the answer of a 16-year-old teen-age boy.
2. An 18-year-old male adolescent said, "They get a sensual pleasure far surpassing the feeling they've had before. They can also talk about it and act proud and cool about their experience."
3. A 15-year-old girl remarked, "I've asked lots of kids to explain it to me, but all they say is, 'you can't really explain it,' or, 'you feel good.'"
4. A 16-year-old female stated, "They escape from reality to escape from their problems."

This question was asked as an attempt to ascertain what non-drug using teens feel drug using teens obtain from drug usage. The largest number of respondents (35% of the boys and 25%

of the girls) felt that the principle effect, or the sought-after desideratum, was escape from their problems, from reality, etc. For this, the non-drug users do not admire the drug users. Later we will compare these data with what the drug using teens think drug usage does for them (p.   ).

Experience, pleasure, "kicks," and "highs" were the second choices; 26 per cent of the boys and 25 per cent of the girls selected these as the assumed reasons why their peers use drugs. These factors agree more with what teens who use drugs, select as their own reasons for drug usage. A discussion of *experience,* is given a prominent part in the last chapter, and will therefore be omitted here.

Other replies include the following:

		Boys	Girls
1.	Cannot understand it	4	9
2.	To be different	6	4
3.	Belonging to a group	2	20
	Total	12	33

The data reveals that 16 per cent of the non-drug using girls felt that "belonging to a group" might be the prompting motive for drug usage. Consistently, it is learned that girls are more inclined to interpersonal or social reasons in their responses. Lastly, a small percentage simply replied they could not assign any reason for drug usage.

Question V. Do you think any of your friends have started to use drugs ?

		Boys	Girls	Percentage
1.	Yes	51	94	80%
2.	No	9	26	20%
	Total	60	120	

Verbatim replies to this question are the following:
1. A 16-year-old girl remarked, "Yea, many of my friends use drugs, and their number is growing."

2. A 15-year-old girl stated, "Yes, even those who I thought never would."
3. A 16-year-old male replied, "Yes, I know quite a few very close friends."
4. "Yes, but it didn't last very long," was the remark of an 18-year-old male.

This question was asked to show simply that many, if not most of the non-drug using teens, were aware that their peers were using drugs.

Question VI. What do you think of your friends who have started to use drugs?

	Boys	*Girls*	*Percentage*
1. Non-judgment ("It's up to them")	25	38	35%
2. They need help	12	7	10%
3. Feel sorry for them	4	38	23%
4. They're dumb ("crazy," "stupid")	3	14	09%
5. Reject them ("I don't want to be around them")	3	11	08%
6. I look down on them	8	6	08%
7. Miscellaneous	5	6	06%
Total	60	120	

Verbatim replies to the above question are as follows:
1. "They have a problem and need help," wrote a 16-year-old male teen.
2. "I think it's a cheap cop-out," wrote a 16-year-old male teen.
3. "I wouldn't be comfortable around a person who used drugs," is the remark of a 17-year-old female.
4. "If they used drugs, I wouldn't think much of them," replied a 16-year-old girl.

The data reveal that many of the non-drug using teens feel that the use of drugs is a matter for the individual to decide, "It's up to them," was frequently given as a response (by 31% of the girls and 41% of the boys). Perhaps theirs is a judgmental/non-judgmental answer.

Girl respondents (31%) replied that they "felt sorry" for their drug using peers, whereas only 6 per cent of the boys gave this same reply. In a sense, the boys were more practical, choosing the entry *they need help.* Twenty per cent of the male respondents chose this reply, but only 5 per cent of the girls. I would assume that the girls feel help is needed, but they *felt sorry,* as a first reaction.

The remainder of the responses may be categorized as follows:

Rejection	Boys	Girls
1. "They're dumb" (crazy, stupid)	3	14
2. "I'd reject them"	3	11
3. "I'd look down on them"	8	6
Total	14	31

Hence, 23 percent of the girls and 17 per cent of the boys respondents indicated strong, negative feelings for their peers who have used drugs.

I interpret a negative response as an *adolescent gap,* at least of a sort. From this finding, the following tentative opinions and some definite conclusions appear justified!

Adults should not group all teen-agers into one category. There are differences among the teen-agers regarding drug usage as well as other important and vital questions. Possible preventive and educational avenues are suggested in this finding.

Question VII. What do you do that helps you to be happy and enjoy yourself or have "an experience," without the use of drugs?

	Boys	Girls	Percentage
1. Friends	7	29	20%
2. Family	7	15	12%
3. Being active	16	7	12%

4. Being myself (self-concept, etc.)	9	29	21%
5. Religion	2	9	07%
6. Boyfriend	0	5	03%
7. Girlfriend	0	0	0%
8. Seeing what drugs do to users.	0	3	02%
9. Enjoying nature	3	3	03%
10. Use of alcohol	3	2	03%
11. Philosophical attitude	7	12	10%
12. Miscellaneous	4	6	09%
Total	60	120	

Verbatim answers to the above question are the following:

1. "I involve myself with school, my community, and life in general," wrote a 16-year-old girl.
2. "I'm just a naturally happy, giggly, immature person who can go into hysterics without any help," replied a 17-year-old girl.
3. A 17-year-old boy stated, "By being myself. This often entails being selfish or self-centered, but it doesn't matter as long as I play one role, myself."
4. A 16-year-old boy remarked, "Striving for a goal, because when I reach the goal, there are my kicks."

The rationale for asking the above question stems from previous research in the area of happiness (1967, 1967A, 1970, 1970A, 1971). Without elaborating the results of this series of studies, it can be simply and accurately stated: If an individual is happy (happiness is "deeper" and more meaningful than sadness) and if he experiences more happy events than sad events, other ways of living (delinquency, alcoholism, mental illness) are neither sought nor needed as avenues of escape, nor paths leading to that elusive psychological colored rainbow, happiness.

In this question, our respondents are freely selecting sources of happiness or experiences, which I assume keep (or at least help) them from resorting to drugs.

The following generic headings might help us in interpreting the data.

Interpersonal	Boys	Girls
1. Friends	7	29
2. Family	7	15
3. Boyfriend (girlfriend)	0	5
Total	14	49

Forty per cent of the girls report that some kind of inter-personal relationship (friend, family, or boyfriend) is not only a source of happiness, as well as "an experience" but also assists in the prevention of the use of drugs. These results agree with the work of Douvan and Adelson (1966) who found that the interpersonal factor is most important in the life of the teen-aged girl. This is a message which parents might profit pondering; the teen-age girl needs a meaningful interpersonal life.

An interpersonal life is also important for the teen-aged boy, since boys selected this entry 23 per cent of the time.

Boys most often chose as a source of prevention against drugs — *being active;* 26 per cent of the boys selected this category. *Being active* is best interpreted as having something to do and this, in turn, suggests an involvement.

The next entry was a bit unexpected: *Being myself.* On the basis of the previous questions, I would have assumed that boys would have selected this category more often than girls. There is some contradictory evidence in the data; at times boys "insist" they can stand on their own two feet and girls "insist" that they lean on others, then suddenly the girls indicate inner-stability. Possible clarification could come from psychological diagnostic material if we knew the personality type responding. Without this information, we can only make suppositions! My own supposition is that what is indicated is what I've seen often in 20 years of marital therapy — the wife "turns out" to be stronger than the husband, who has resorted to some kind of crutch. Perhaps exposure of the male to many situations demanding a constant role causes a facade or crutch to emerge. Females have many chances to rehearse or practice different roles; thus the facade or crutch may not develop.

The category *philosophical attitude* refers to a reflective orientation, the ability to think, to ponder, to question; to wonder is the beginning of wisdom, according to the ancient Greek philosophers. Here we have 11 per cent of the boys and 10 per cent of the girls who chose philosophical attitude as a source of happiness, as well as "an experience." Perhaps parents could instill this type of attitude into family discussions. In our family we have found it useful to have "themes" or "ideas," which we think about for the week. Surely, drugs are not necessary to introduce one into the world of ideas, flights of fantasy, or reflection.

Other sources of happiness are religion, music, sports, and nature. At times, other unhealthy outlets are chosen — alcohol.

In summary, 180 teen-agers (120 girls and 60 boys) who have not used drugs, have provided the reader with some potentially useful ideas for prevention, education, and treatment which could lead the reader and his parents (or peers) into an "experience."

The non-drug using teen-ager as reflected by the present respondents suggests the following "typical people." He is an individual who feels no need for drugs, either presently or in the future. Should he become involved in drugs, the sources of help as projected are competent professional help, or a peer *not* using drugs, parents, or from within the self.

A divided opinion exists regarding why their peers use drugs, namely, they feel it is either escape from life or a drive toward experience. They also differ regarding their feelings concerning their drug using peers. The largest group reflect a nonjudgmental attitude, while others felt rejecting and critical.

As the respondents reflected on what has helped them remain drug free, the principal reasons which emerged were the following: friends, family, meaningful activity, and self-reliance (or rationale/self-respect).

Chapter III

RESEARCH RESULTS WITH
DRUG ABUSING TEEN-AGERS

THIS chapter is a report on (25 boys and 55 girls) drug abusing teen-agers who state that they are not only using drugs currently, but plan to continue to use drugs.

The term *drug abusing* is synonymous with *drug dependent*. For a definition of drug dependent, I will use that of the W.H.O. Technical Report (1967) which states,

> ... a state arising from repeated administration of a drug on a periodic or continuous basis. . . . .
>
> Individuals may become dependent upon a wide variety of chemical substances covering the whole range of pharmacodynamic effects from stimulation to depression. All these drugs have at least one effect in common. They are capable of creating a state of mind in certain individuals which is termed psychic-dependence. This is a psychic drive which requires periodic or chronic administrations of the drug for pleasure or to avoid discomfort.

As in Chapter II on non-drug using teen-agers, this applies to drug abusing teen-agers of this chapter, the research revolves around a series of slightly modified questions.

Blum and associates, *Students and Drugs* (1970), report on their research with college drug using students. The reader who is interested in that age population will find Blum's work a valuable point of reference.

Blum and associates comment that their study mentions that some external data was obtained regarding intensive versus less intensive college drug using students, but ". . . these are external descriptions and do not tell us how different students experienced the drugs taken either in terms of specific effects or in nonspecific ones, including the meanings attached to one experience."

In the present study I have attempted to give a partial answer to the subjective experience given to drug use.

As in Chapter II tabulation of entries, verbatim statements from the respondents, and discussion of the findings, follow the previous question.

Question I: At what age did you start using drugs?

Age	Boys	Girls	Percentage
11	-	2	03%
12	1	3	06%
13	3	10	21%
14	7	11	30%
15	6	7	21%
16	8	3	19%
Total	25	35	

The same sampled population (urban high school students attending middle class, white, neighborhoods) were used for the data reported in this chapter.

My long term (12 years) as a consultant with a girls delinquent institution appears appropriate at this point. Often the trouble started for girls at the ages of 13 and 14. The age of puberty seems to trigger a rebellion against their parents and school. It is the time also for experimentation with so many things — drugs being just one.

Thus, the age of beginning drug usage for girls is earlier than for boys.

If my assumption is valid, junior high school (7th and 8th grade) is the critical time. Therefore, preventive measures should be pushed harder at this time. Special classes which involve parents, specialists, and students would seem to be of benefit.

Question II: What kind or type of drugs did you use?

Type of Drug	Boys	Girls	Percentage
1. Marijuana (only)	5	7	20%
2. Three or more types of drugs (but *not* heroin)	20	27	79%
3. Three or more types of drugs (including heroin)	0	1	01%
Total	25	35	

From this data, we learn that generally the teen-age drug user takes a number of drugs. Our finding, that often the adolescent takes more than one drug, conflicts with the statements made in the W.H.O. Technical Report (1967).

Question III: How long have you used drugs?

Length of Time	Boys	Girls	Percentage
6 months	1	3	07%
9 months	1	1	01%
1 year	10	7	29%
1½ years	3	5	14%
2 years	8	12	34%
3 years	1	6	12%
4 years	1	1	02%
Total	25	35	

An inspection of the above table reveals that the majority of the sampled population has been using drugs for a lengthy time, over one year. In fact, 40 per cent of the teen-age boy respondents report having used drugs for over two years. Whereas, 34 per cent of the girls report having used drugs for the same length of time.

Question IV: Why won't you stop taking drugs?

Content	Boys	Girls	Percentage
1. The "pay-off" is good, ("I like the experience")	14	13	45%
2. No harm	3	4	12%
3. Escape	4	3	12%
4. "Kicks" (fun)	1	4	08%
5. Just do not want to	3	5	13%
6. Helps spiritual growth	0	1	01%
7. Slowing down (using drugs)	0	3	05%
8. Miscellaneous	0	2	03%
Total	25	35	

Verbatim examples to the above question are the following:

1. A 17-year-old girl wrote, "My mind has expanded, so I think clearer in all thought areas."
2. Another 17-year-old girl explained, "I really don't know — for everything to go my way, I guess."
3. "No harm" is the reply of a 16-year-old boy.
4. "Speed and LSD, I have quit because I became convinced they were dangerous. Pot has not been proven harmful and doesn't appear to be harming me."

The majority of drug using teen-agers state that the reason they use drugs is because of the *experience* which I refer to as the *pay-off;* 56 per cent of the boys and 37 per cent of the girls select this entry — they claim the "pay-off" is their principle reason for drug usage.

If you recall the data from non-drug using teens when asked to respond to the question, "Why do you think teen-agers use drugs?" they thought that *escape* was the principle reason.

It is difficult for me to assume any segment of a population may assign "poor" reasons for their activity. It has been found, moreover, that certain people within a well-defined group find it difficult at times to "assign" themselves scholastically to their reference group.

For instance, Cudrin (1970) asked 42 convicts in a federal penitentiary, "Do you consider yourself a criminal?" The majority defined *criminal* in such a manner as to exclude themselves.

In addition to the above considerations the concept of an *experience* appears paramount as a motivating reason for the continued use of drugs by our respondents. Since this notion looms so prominent, I have postponed a discussion of the concept of *experience,* until the final chapter.

At this juncture, it suffices to note that *"experience"* is the principal reported reason for the continued use of drugs. Another entry is *escape;* some of the teens frankly mentioned this motivation.

Therapy of some form certainly should be substituted. "Kicks" as a principal reason or motivation for drug usage is given only by a few respondents — 2 boys and 4 girls.

Salisbury and Fertig (1969) mention several motives behind the use of drugs by the young. They first list "curiosity," then "drugs are medicine," and a third item is that "drugs are fun." In the authors' interviews with teen-age users, the most common response to the question of "why?" was, "It's fun!"

S. Cohen (*The Drug Dilemma: A Partial Solution*) writes, "Many of those attracted to the drug experience, suffer from anhedonism, the inability to derive pleasure from ordinary existence alienation; the inability to find a meaning within or outside oneself."

The present research rather clearly suggests that the teen-age drug user employs drugs for an experience — of closeness, of intimacy, of relationship, of getting "lost" in an experience. Lennard and his associates (1971) make the statement:

> Despite the fact that the ingestion of psychoactive agents appears to open up sensory modalities and to facilitate interaction by dissolving boundaries, by aligning expectations, and by attuning modalities of communication, it appears to us that the interaction thus facilitated does not have quite the same properties as drug-free interactions. It is, in our view, more of a pseudointeraction than an authentic one.

Secondly, a distinction must be made between "for fun" and "anhedonism." The former is impulsive; in the latter, there is an inability to find or experience pleasure, or an inability to be happy, and this is far more serious. In my mind it is one of the omens of schizophrenia, and a current indication of this emotional disorder. May's (1969) book, *Love and Will,* includes a chapter entitles "Our Schizoid World," suggesting that the present culture drives many individuals toward a schizoid life.

Regarding the hedonic factor, Rinzler and Shapiro (1968) have described what they believe to be a new clinical syndrome, namely the "wrist-cutting" phenomenon. Among the clinical descriptions of wrist-cutting, the authors mention, (aside from pertaining to young females) "Their fluid and unstable social lives usually involve frequent and varied drug use . . . " Rinzler and Shapiro conclude that these patients feel alive only if they *feel,* "I feel, therefore, I am"; and their blood running from their wrists prove that they are alive.

A model advanced by Giammatteo (1969) describes a circular situation. The teen-ager thinks, then acts (DO) or does something and gets a feeling (FEEL). After several rehearsals of an event such

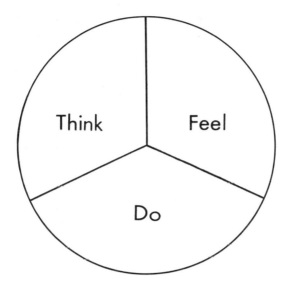

as drug using rituals, the teen stops getting the urge to think, but merely acts or does (DO) something to get the feeling. After repeated desensitizing experiences, the feel is lost and a teen remains a doer, who ritualistically behaves without thinking or feeling.

Question V: What would you speculate, might help you to stop taking drugs?

	Content	*Boys*	*Girls*	*Percentage*
1.	My decision	9	8	29%
2.	Nothing (will not stop)	12	7	32%
3.	It is difficult to say	1	3	07%
4.	Different environment	0	2	02%
5.	Alcohol	1	2	05%
6.	Different friends	1	3	06%
7.	Family	0	1	01%
8.	Law	0	1	01%
9.	Fear	1	5	10%
10.	Miscellaneous	0	3	05%
	Total	25	35	

Verbatim responses to this question are as follows:

1. An 18-year-old girl replied, "It's a hard question to answer. At times, I don't even want them, other times I don't think I could make it without them. It depends on how things are going, I guess. If I know there is something I have to do; something serious that will affect my life, I stay away from drugs, knowing it gives me an, "I don't care" attitude."
2. A 17-year-old boy reflected, "If I were convinced that pot was indeed harmful, I would quit immediately."
3. A 17-year-old girl stated, "Nothing but my own will power."
4. A 16-year-old boy stated, "Probably if all my friends weren't interested in dope, but I am not planning to lay off."

An examination of the responses indicates that two entries contain the majority of responses:

1.	My decision	36% boys	23% girls
2.	Nothing (will not stop)	48% boys	20% girls
		84% boys	43% girls

Both of these entries could be placed under the generic heading of *I decide to stop or not to stop.* Apparently, this factor has often been overlooked or placed in relatively minor importance; but it is crucially important that an individual wants to stop — drinking, crying, getting angry, being dependent, criminal actions, etc.

The results of therapy are often hampered, if not outright negated, because the "victim" implies he is "powerless" to do such and such. Whereas, the truth of the matter is, he simply chooses what he wants to do.

It would appear to me that the following is an accurate evaluation of youthful drug-abusers:

1. Some of the teen-agers simply want to remain on drugs.
2. Some are hooked (dependent) and additional help (therapy) is needed.
3. Some think they could stop if they *wanted* to "get off drugs."
4. If the "pay-off" is excellent (as subjectively experienced

therefore valued) the decision to stop drug use will be postponed.

Frequently, the decision to use drugs emerges either from our environmental pressure ("everyone else is using drugs"; or their close friends use drugs; or their boyfriend or girlfriend) uses drugs. This could be termed a "sociogeneric" drug abuser.

Another type of youthful drug-abuser could be termed "psychogeneric." This implies that the decision to use drugs, stemmed from discouragement, depression, loneliness, etc. Regarding this latter category of drug-abuse, Robins and associates (1970), in their study of drug abuse, arrived at a number of conclusions, among which were the following:

> In short, drugs have been used because they give pleasure and at the same time permit the continued justification of failure to fit into more socially demanding roles.

These authors point out that before drug use many drug abusers felt unable to live up to expectations and turned to drug use as a way of expressing rebellion against school, parents, and society. Giammatteo's concepts of restructuring what is around you in fantasy if you cannot do it in "real" life is applicable.

These theories and my experience lead me to conclude that this type of drug abuser is more difficult to help. The one who still continues with his goals (education, work, etc.) does not have to reorientate his whole life or restructure it once he stops taking drugs.

Question VI: Do you wish you had not started taking drugs?

	Content	*Boys*	*Girls*	*Percentage*
1.	Yes	1	2	03%
2.	No	18	25	72%
3.	Everything but marijuana	6	5	19%
4.	I think so	0	3	05%
	Total	25	35	

Verbatim replies to the above question are as follows:
   1. A 17-yeay-old male who had used drugs for two years wrote, "No, during my trips, I have experienced things that other people will never see."

2. A 16-year-old male replied, "If I didn't smoke grass, I would drink, which is a poorer habit. When I get older, I will have to stop grass, but someone that started on alcohol will go right on drinking until he dies."
3. A 17-year-old female stated, "No, dope opened up my unexplored realms of consciousness. Subtler and subtler field of matter and energy."
4. An 18-year-old girl said, "Sometimes, I suppose it depends on the frame of mind I'm in at the time."

The above results are what one would suspect — if an individual persists in an activity, he must justify or rationalize his behavior. We do note a distinction being made with some of the drug users; only marijuana is used, having suffered some type of negative effect from the other drugs.

It might be instructive to refer to the remarks of Lennard and associates (1971). They employed the example of Freud, who used cocaine and later introduced a friend, Ernst Fleischl Marxou, to the use of cocaine. Years later Freud refused to take any type of drugs and suffered greatly because of introducing his friend to cocaine. Lennard and associates state, "when confronted by the argument that it is after all the user of drugs who, on the basis of experience, is the best judge of drug effects and drug dangers."

Question VII: What do you think you are getting out of drugs?

Content	Boys	Girls	Percentage
1. Experiencing more	17	24	69%
2. Love and friendship	0	3	05%
3. Escape	4	2	10%
4. Kicks	2	5	12%
5. Peace	0	1	01%
6. Confusion	1	0	01%
7. Self-knowledge	1	0	01%
Total	25	35	

Verbatim examples to the above questions are as follows:
1. A 16-year-old girl wrote, "Lots of friends, new perspective on religion, weight loss (every so often), feeling of elation —

that I'm the best and sometimes it's good to feel that way. Dope gives me a peace that I never knew before. I can be happy when I'm sad and vice versa. It may be strange, but when I do a speed run, I feel like a goody-goody and it's a good feeling. I do everything right. Dope makes me a beautiful person to myself."

2. A 17-year-old girl said, "Nothing, I just have some fun with friends, something different. Dope is only a crutch — out of the ordinary."

3. A 17-year-old boy explained, "Not to escape reality. It broadens every point of life and makes it enjoyable."

4. An 18-year-old male remarked, "I get pure relaxation and enjoyment out of grass; it helps me to see things better."

In a way *Question VII* is a replication of *Question IV* (Why won't you stop taking drugs?). Essentially, the same data is obtained from the present question. The majority of the respondents (68% of the girls and 68% of the boys) point out that "experience" (pay-off) is essentially the principal reason for taking drugs. The principle effect reported is that of "experiencing more." Since this concept will be discussed in the final chapter, it will not be touched on here.

The reply given by a 16-year-old girl respondent (. . . I feel like a goody-goody and it's a good feeling. I do everything right. Dope makes me a beautiful person to myself.) is intriguing to me. I have a number of speculations about the outcome, one of the speculations is that she might begin to have some of the problems of Alice, in Lewis Carroll's (1866) *Through the Looking Glass*. Most readers will recall Alice's struggle with Tweedledum and Tweedledee — insisting that she was real. "I am real," said Alice and began to cry. "You won't make yourself a bit realer by crying," said Tweedledee, "There's nothing to cry about." When Alice mentioned her tears, Tweedledum remarked, they weren't "real tears."

Is our respondent going to have difficulty in figuring out which self (drug or drug free) is the real self? This is the "turned on" child.

Question VIII: Would you advise other teen-agers to take drugs?

Content	Boys	Girls	Percentage
1. It's up to them	15	18	55%
2. No	2	9	19%
3. Yes	3	3	10%
4. Yes (marijuana only)	6	5	17%
Total	25	35	

Verbatim replies to the above question are as follows:
1. A 17-year-old girl replied, "I think everyone should smoke marijuana *once* in their lives. I feel I can control myself and if some kids are smoking dope, and I don't want any, I don't have any."
2. A 17-year-old girl said, "No, just because I cannot become addicted, doesn't mean they won't."
3. An 18-year-old male responded, "I think if they are old enough, they should try marijuana, if they want to, but as to LSD and speed, no."
4. "I could care less if they did or did not. I don't advertize drugs," wrote a 16-year-old teen-age boy.

Masterson (1967) compared 101 adolescent patients with 101 controls. Controls consisted of adolescents from the community "who had never been seen for consultation or treatment by a psychologist, psychiatrist, or social worker." Patients and controls were matched for age, grade, sex, race, religion, and type of school attended.

The adolescents were interviewed separately by two psychiatrists, for one hour each. The first psychiatrist conducted a standard examination, the second psychiatrist guided his hour along a devised questionnaire.

Some results which appear pertinent for our purposes are the following:
1. Anxiety, depression, and immature personality were found as fairly similar in the two groups, a substantial portion in both groups had anxiety and depression.
2. The patient group showed differences in schizophrenia, acting out and sexual difficulty.

The average teen-ager will be bothered, or at least experience amounts of anxiety and depression. If he cannot tolerate these, seemingly "normal" ingredients in his life process, drugs will hinder him by avoiding the growth patterns and inner conflicts, normal and natural for him. There might result an "unnatural" yearning to escape all conflict and hassles whether internal or external.

The respondents, who are using drugs and insist that they plan on continuing to use drugs, present a typical picture of early drug use involving use of more than one drug and justification of the usage around two principal avenues — the "pay-off" is good (this implies some kind of experience) or there's no harm, and it is fun and an escape hatch.

Thus usage of drugs appears to be a deeply entrenched element, many clinging to it either in a stubborn or rationalized fashion.

Chapter IV

RESEARCH RESULTS WITH FORMER TEEN-AGED DRUG ABUSERS

 T HIS chapter is a report on teen-agers (35 boys and 50 girls) who for a period of time were drug abusers, but who have stopped using drugs.

As in the two former chapters, this chapter will revolve around the data collected from a series of questions. The format will include the results from each question, verbatim responses to the question, and discussion of the findings when feasible comparisons with questions noted in Chapters II and III will be made.

Question I: At what age did you start to use drugs?

Age	Boys	Girls	Percentage
12	1	6	08%
13	6	9	19%
14	14	16	35%
15	9	14	27%
16	4	4	09%
17	1	1	01%
Total	35	50	

It can be seen that the obtained data from this question does not differ significantly from the data so obtained from teen-agers who will not stop using drugs. The critical period is the early teens. The time, therefore, for drug preventive methods should preceed this period.

Question II: What kind of drugs did you use?

Type of Drug	Boys	Girls	Percentage
1. Marijuana	9	8	20%
2. LSD	0	1	01%

3. Three or more kinds,

    but *not* heroin   25   39   76%

4. Three or more kinds

    including heroin   1   2   02%

        Total   ——   ——
                                        35   50

This data confirms, essentially, the data obtained in the previous section; that is, the teen-agers sampled use a variety of drugs. Some (16% of the girls and 26% of the boys) used only marijuana; this group of "stoppers" do have a higher percentage of "marijuana only."

Question III: How long did you use drugs?

Period of Time	Boys	Girls	Percentage
3 months	5	5	12%
6 months	8	12	24%
1 year	6	12	21%
1½ years	4	11	17%
2 years	6	5	13%
3 years	3	4	08%
4 years	3	1	04%
Total	35	50	

Comparing these results with those obtained in the former section, it can be seen that "stoppers" often use drugs for shorter periods of time — 3 and 6 months. Assuming that the sampled population rather accurately reflects a white, middle class, high school student from a metropolitan area, what is emerging might be rather significant.

If teen drug users can be "gathered" for help after 3 or 6 months of drug use, they might be more likely to accept help.

No data are included, in the present study, on those teens who have a few "joints" of marijuana and have stopped. This type of data would be important. A case illustration may serve as a useful purpose in this matter.

For instance, Joe, a 17-year-old boy related to me,

> I tried grass a few times, but didn't like it. It gave me a dead feeling, like nothing was happening — lifeless, and my mouth was dry. I'd say something to my friends and it was as if I was thinking it and not saying it. My friend, Bill, and I were going to use acid, but we wised up. I haven't used drugs since (2 years ago). I just don't like to do things to make me feel different. I like to feel straight and normal.

The number of experimenters and the reasons they have stopped after a few "tries" would be fascinating information. My hunch is that combined motives would be operative: a) not gaining much from the experience, b) no one encouraging them to keep trying, c) guilt about the use of drugs, d) other incentives or interests (people, activity, school).

Question IV: Why did you stop using drugs?

	Content	Boys	Girls	Percentage
1.	Getting little or no "pay-off"	10	23	39%
2.	Psychological (or emotional) problems	10	3	16%
3.	Physical effects	3	4	08%
4.	Fear (real bummers, friend's death, etc.)	5	5	12%
5.	Effects of friends	0	2	02%
6.	Busted or fear of being busted	1	5	07%
7.	Religion	1	1	02%
8.	Boy (girl) friend	1	2	03%
9.	Family	1	1	02%
10.	Meditation	1	0	01%
11.	Miscellaneous	2	4	07%
	Total	35	50	

Verbatim responses to the above question are as follows:

1. A 17-year-old girl stated, "Guilt. I was seeing my friends get hung up on drugs; seeing the ones I'd started on drugs get busted. I was getting so I couldn't take the crashing, so I'd get ripped again. It was costing too much. I was lying to

myself; I realized it was only an escape."
2. A 16-year-old girl wrote, "I went on a bad trip while on LSD. It scared me because I couldn't come down. That's when I decided to quit."
3. A 17-year-old boy said, "Just deciding to stay off; it's not worth it."
4. "No satisfaction, no control. I believe grass had an adverse effect on my mind and body," are the comments of a 16-year-old boy.

Perhaps we can get a clearer picture of the results by utilizing the generic heading: "No Pay-Off."

No Pay-Off	*Boys*	*Girls*
1. Little or no "pay-off"	10	23
2. Psychological or emotional problems	10	3
3. Physical effects	3	4
4. Fear ("real bummer")	5	5
Total	28	35

In other words, 80 per cent of the boys and 70 per cent of the girls answered that "lack of pay-off" was the prompting reason for stopping the use of drugs. These data point up sharply and clearly, some important psychological facts:
1. Most teen-agers will stop using drugs when the results are unsatisfactory.
2. If the results are "good" (as noted in the previous section), they will continue to use drugs.

Other reasons for stopping the use of drugs include the following:
1. Fear of being apprehended.
2. Effects on friends.
3. Religion.

Question V: How long have you been off drugs?

Period of Time	*Boys*	*Girls*	*Percentage*
2 months	7	9	19%

3 months	8	12	24%
6 months	10	9	23%
9 months	4	13	20%
1 year	5	6	12%
2 years	1	1	02%
Total	35	50	

Perhaps some of the respondents have not stopped taking drugs a sufficient period of time to qualify them as "stoppers." Yet, on the other hand, I know of no other studies concerned with length of time regarding this issue.

Question VI: What has helped you to stay off drugs?

	Content	Boys	Girls	Percentage
1.	Will power (or self determination)	15	7	26%
2.	Boyfriend	0	6	07%
3.	Girlfriend	1	0	01%
4.	Avoid people who use drugs	1	5	07%
5.	Family	2	4	07%
6.	Fear (of insanity, etc.)	1	7	09%
7.	Therapy	5	3	09%
8.	No "pay-off"	3	6	10%
9.	Religion	3	3	07%
10.	Friends (girl)	0	6	07%
11.	Friends (boy)	1	0	01%
12.	Miscellaneous	3	3	07%
	Total	35	50	

Verbatim examples of the above question are the following:

1. A 17-year-old girl wrote, "I met a boy who was older and seemed like a dream come true. I didn't want him to know I took drugs; he found out. I had a long talk with him, plans for the future . . ." She has been off 6 months.

2. A 17-year-old girl stated, "I think the fact that I faced myself and have become honest with myself is the major cause. Also, a friend of mine has stopped and that has helped."

3. A 17-year-old boy stated, "A feeling that I don't need them. I just quit." He had used drugs (marijuana, LSD, and mescaline) for two years.

The intent of this question, as you can quickly surmise, was to help in the treatment modalities for youthful drug users.

The results clearly indicate that boys (43%) report that self-determination, including the ideas suggested by it (ego, strength, will power), were the critical factors in helping them to stay off drugs. Girls do not endorse this factor as frequently as boys as the critical factor. Perhaps it can be safely and accurately stated that the two necessary conditions for the stopping and the remaining off drugs are the following:

1. No "pay-off."
2. Decision (will power) not to continue the use of drugs.

In other words, one's decision not to use drugs is enhanced (given greater consideration) because there is little "pay-off." A similar motive is operative for the girls, but not to the same frequency. It appears that one "strong" or "crucial" condition is sufficient.

GIRLS' MOTIVATION AGAINST DRUG USE

1.	Boyfriend	12%
2.	Fear of insanity	14%
3.	Help of girlfriends	12%
4.	No "pay-off"	12%
5.	Avoidance of peers using drugs	10%

What has emerged from this question, I think, are leads which can be utilized in the treatment aspects of drug users. The therapist cannot "supply" a boy friend but it would seem worthwhile to involve girlfriends of teen-age girls attempting to remain from drug usage. In fact, I find it useful to present to any patient results of research which have helped other patients. I would suggest that the present data be shared.

Question VII: What might happen to start you taking drugs again?

	Content	Boys	Girls	Percentage
1.	Nothing (will not start)	15	15	36%
2.	Emotional problems	6	13	23%
3.	Uncertain	6	7	16%
4.	Depression (just not caring)	0	5	06%
5.	Wrong crowd	5	4	10%
6.	Family problems	0	2	02%
7.	Something tragic happening	0	1	01%
8.	Poor grades	1	1	01%
9.	Induction in service (being sent to Viet Nam)	1	0	01%
10.	Miscellaneous	1	2	03%
	Total	35	50	

Verbatim examples to the above question are the following:

1. A 17-year-old boy remarked, "I imagine nothing. I feel that I'm smart enough to know when to stop. I'd never take anything again . . ."

2. "It's impossible that I would ever take drugs again," wrote a 17-year-old boy.

3. A 15-year-old girl insisted, "I would probably die or kill myself. I couldn't hurt my parents or myself again."

4. An 18-year-old girl wrote, "If I would lose trust in the people I think now are my friends, I would turn back on drugs, or if some time I would get upset and have nobody to turn to, I could go to my friends who do take drugs and ask them to get me stoned. If I again would feel like nobody, knowing that I am unloved and unwanted, I would turn to drugs again."

The purpose of this question was to obtain factors which might reactivate the use of drugs by teens who had stopped. It seems to me that some encouraging and significant material emerged. The majority of respondents (45% of the boys and 30% of the girls) report "nothing," "I won't start again," indicating that once off drugs, things are either so much better or they recall the difficulties when using drugs, that it simply is not worth returning to drug usage again.

It is my impression that these findings are both hopeful and helpful. Hopeful, in that the drug problem can be defeated and "stay licked" by teens. Helpful in that it can be influencial to those teens struggling to stop taking drugs and remain off drugs.

The other respondents are not as certain as the examples cited above, suggesting that certain conditions could possibly reactivate the use of drugs; and the respondents indicate some of the conditions.

Possible factors which might lead to drug use again:

		Boys	*Girls*
1.	Emotional problems	17%	26%
2.	Uncertain	17%	14%
3.	Wrong crowd	14%	08%

These findings can be utilized in treatment with teens. Both therapist and teen patient should be aware of the above, and attempts to overcome the drug problem must be tried;

Question VIII: Do you wish you had not started taking drugs?

	Content	*Boys*	*Girls*	*Percentage*
1.	Yes	15	18	39%
2.	No	17	25	50%
3.	Cannot say	3	7	11%
	Total	35	50	

Verbatim replies to this question are the following:
1. A 16-year-old girl said,"Yes, I feel if I never would have tried them, I wouldn't have the memories of what they can do for me when I happen to be the least little bit down or even when I'm just looking for excitement."
2. A 17-year-old girl replied, "No, I now know I can't depend on material means to achieve what I want. I can't say I haven't learned; having the strength to stand up to my

friends and quit drugs really gave me self-respect. Now I'm ready to help others, where before I couldn't help myself. It made me understand I've got to start at home with myself and relatives before I help others. The drugs themselves didn't help, but after I quit, all this occurred."

3. A 17-year-old boy reflected, "No, it's good to know what it's like. I'm glad I did know — I won't always be wondering."

4. A 16-year-old boy replied, "No, it was an experience which I will never regret, though I'll never do it again."

As can be seen from the results of the above table, the respondents are somewhat evenly divided concerning the question, "Do you wish you had not started taking drugs?"

The responses indicated the following:

1. If a former teen-age drug user recalls the "bad things" (memories, scares) he or she will most likely reply in the affirmative.

2. If a former, teen-age drug user reacts, "Well, I did learn something," he or she are more apt to reply in the negative.

Question IX: Would you advise other teens to take drugs?

Content	Boys	Girls	Percentage
1. No	10	32	50%
2. Yes	2	2	05%
3. Marijuana only	8	5	15%
4. It is up to them	15	11	30%
Total	35	50	

Verbatim replies to the above question are as follows:

1. A 16-year-old girl stated, "Never! I'm very, very much against drugs because of how much of my life I've wasted. One year is a lot."

2. A 17-year-old girl replied, "No, so many of my friends are so insecure and paranoid, perhaps for life, because of drugs."

3. A 15-year-old boy wrote, "No! Too many kids go from pot to other things. Not because it's physical, they are just looking for a bigger kick."

4. A 16-year-old teen-age male said, "No, nobody needs them. Most people have the will power, so they don't need to use them. Most of all, don't do it just because others are."

The results from this question fall into the following two headings:

1. It is up to each person to make a decision.

>   24% of the girls

>   43% of the boys

2. No.

>   64% of the girls

>   28% of the boys

The respondents seem to be saying, "I'm not going to advise others to use drugs — I wish they wouldn't, but it's really up to each individual to decide." Another large segment of the respondents definitely would advise other young people not to use drugs. The verbatim quotes give some of the reasons for their feelings.

A somewhat typical profile of a former teen-age drug user, as emerging from our respondents, suggests that the "pay-off" (reward) was judged to be too little, coupled with growing fears and emotional problems. This factor, when joined by a firm determination (will power or ego-strength) are rather effective in a stout commitment of never returning to drug use again. But there are some problems which could trigger, once again, the use of drugs.

Many of our respondents would not advise their peers to start using drugs. In general, the impact of data leaves one with hope that something can be done to help youthful drug abusers.

Aristotle said it well several centuries ago, "Hope is the dream of a waking man." Perhaps our dreams can now turn to expectations and plans. The young people, time and again, offer suggestion after suggestion, fact after fact, of what has helped them. Consequently, it appears that from research of the present type, practical suggestions emerge. Suggestions which do not have to be "translated" from the laboratory (either animal laboratory or from "controlled" studies of individuals in simulated situations) to real life. Rather, the data are supplied by real people, in real situations.

The following two chapters will implement the data which have evolved from our findings.

Thus the "leads" have already been applied.

Chapter V

A TEEN-AGER'S SUBJECTIVE
APPRAISAL OF DRUG USE, THERAPY,
AND SUBSEQUENT LIFE STYLE

T*HIS chapter was written by a 17-year-old girl, whom I saw in treatment for a period of six months. One year after termination of treatment I asked Jane (fictitious name) to, "Make some remarks regarding drugs, therapy, and your subsequent life." The following chapter was Jane's response.*

Jane was an attractive teen-aged girl, quite bright, with a devotion for reading, often got "hooked" on her most recent book and its ideas. She had better than average verbal ability.

I will not relate more, but allow Jane to unfold herself, and her story.

This chapter is a form of "data-gathering" which hopefully, can furnish insights, understanding, and help for other teen-agers using drugs. There are, in short, other "Janes" and other "Johns."

Different people use dope in different ways and for different purposes. It's a purely individual thing. And the story of my use of drugs is my story, not the story of a whole generation. Because dope was by and large a good experience for me, I used to assume that it was so for others. It came as a shock to find that that wasn't true, that in fact, for some people dope is a very bad thing.

Many things led up to my first experience with drugs. I come from a middle class home, I led a middle class life and had basically middle class values when I reached high school. High school was a new world, a new challenge. Most of the changes that occured within me that first year were the direct result of a class I was taking from a young sensitive teacher on world religions and comparative ethics. I had never challenged any of the values that I had assimilated from my sheltered environment in my early adolescence. Suddenly I was presented with brand new conceptions of reality, conceptions which were vastly different from the reality I was born and raised in. Becoming aware of, and trying to understand the different sects of Christianity, the major world religions, and current philosophical movements like existentialism broadened my world explosively. Suddenly I wasn't so sure that my reality was the only or transcendent one. There were questions, myriads of them. And as I began to question and to grow, a few things became obvious to me. My life began to take on a new meaning. Even if I didn't know exactly what I believed or where I was heading, I did know that to be really living, I had to be constantly changing and growing. Even if I didn't have a clear goal in mind, I was at least sure of the general path I was to take.

I remember spending a lot of time that first year trying to understand the odd-looking, odd-talking, odd-acting people called hippies. Their reality was different. They looked, acted, talked, and thought differently. And somehow their freedom, their bizarreness, their mysteriousness attracted me. My first-hand contacts with them were limited that first year although I had plenty of opportunities to make contacts. I thought a lot about the weird things they said that sounded absolutely foreign to me. After battling things out in my head some, I began to understand little bits and pieces of what they were saying.

My whole world was in a turmoil at the time. I had no answers, just a lot of questions. Since I had no identity, no self-concept based on reality, I was particularly vulnerable to the dreamy, too-good-to-be-true values and culture of the alienated youth. Part of me wanted to establish a self-identity through alignment with the group identity of the hippies. Back when I first started using drugs, anyone who was a drug user was associated in my mind with the hippie ideal. Open-mindedness, freedom, spontaneity, love. For me to try marijuana symbolized my closeness to those ideals. But the use of drugs symbolized more than an affirmation, it also symbolized a negation; of society, the status quo, of everything that was considered oppressive.

Marijuana, or grass as it is commonly called, was something I was frightened of, but I soon learned that it was not the killer drug I had been led to believe it was. The assertions made by grass users that it was no worse than alcohol was supported by medical evidence. I knew I wouldn't be hooked if I tried it once, and that experimentation was going on all over which seemed to make my experimentation sanctionable. Several of my friends had tried it and they had been very positive about the experience. I was, to put it simply, curious. Convinced that it wasn't dangerous, I decided I wanted to try it.

My opportunity came unexpectedly. I was riding on a ski club bus on my way to the mountain when my friend Mary, pulled out some brownies.

"Want some brownies?" she asked.

"Sure." I said without thinking anything of it.

Then she leaned over and whispered in my ear, "They have marijuana in them."

I looked at the brownie in my hand with facination and uttered an astonished "Oh!". I was on edge, knowing that if I ate some brownies, I would have to face whatever came. But my curiosity was stronger than my lingering fear and I popped one in my mouth. They tasted like perfectly normal brownies, the only apparent difference being the texture. I kept on finding myself chewing stems and seeds. I remember feeling nervous for some time, not knowing what to expect. We continued our conversation and finished up the brownies. I became so engrossed in our conversation that I completely forgot about the significance of what I had just done.

Soon I found myself giggling and laughing with Mary at practically everything that caught our attention. It was as if behind each one of her statements lay myriads of levels of subtlety. Some observation she might make wouldn't be taken at face value, rather my mind would seem to travel down a path, understanding the observation in a million different ways. One can make some of the most interesting, original, or even ludicrous connections when stoned. I remember a simple observation of hers on a tree leaving me with a flash of insight into her way of perceiving reality, I wouldn't just hear her say something on a superficial level; I would feel it, taste it, really understand it. Or think I understood it.

We were so intensely involved in our relating that the time simply seemed to fly. What seemed like ten minutes was an hour and a half. I don't remember exactly how it began, but sitting next to each other on the bus seat we started to gently hit each other in slow motion. That we were in slow motion we weren't really aware of, but back and forth we'd go, each recoiling (in slow motion) from the other's touch as if really hit. I don't know how long this had been going on, probably about five minutes, when I, reacting to a blow of hers, lost my balance and proceeded to fall off the seat and down to the floor — all in perfectly controlled slow motion.

When I looked up, with tears in my eyes from laughing so hard, I saw that practically the whole bus was watching us and probably had been for awhile. It wasn't until that moment that I fully realized I was stoned. I quickly regained my seat and we did our best to start looking and acting as normal as everyone else. For practically that whole bus ride, neither of us had been aware that there was a busload of people surrounding us. As we began to realize this, I experienced for the first time a feeling that I was to experience many times again. The unpleasant feeling of paranoia.

Paranoia almost always goes with drug use. There are a lot of paranoid kids walking around right now. Taking drugs is illegal. That means that a drug user is a criminal. It is no small thing to be caught in possession of grass. To the individual drug user, his drug use means that if he is caught, the whole legal system of this country is his enemy. The drug user who can maintain is lucky. To maintain means the ability to keep your cool and remain undetected while stoned in the presence of straight people. It also means being able to maintain control of yourself while stoned so that you don't freak out. Maintaining is a matter of survival. Those that can't maintain either get caught, or they get so frightened that they quit drugs, thinking the hassle and paranoia aren't worth it.

To be able to use drugs and maintain in the presence of non-drug users requires the development of certain qualities of a good con artist. One must learn to mask his true feelings and reactions. He must learn to operate in two worlds at any given time in a sort of conscious and deliberate schizophrenia. To be able to mask true feelings in order to impress straight people of your normalacy requires a certain dishonesty that becomes an intregal part of any drug users life. It's an odd and unpleasant sensation to be stoned and desperately trying to determine what to do to look normal and inconspicous, especially when you feel very conspicous and abnormal.

To be paranoid means to not be sure of your ability to maintain, to feel sure that everyone detects your stonedness. Hence, furtive glances at bystanders and over-reactions to gestures or looks by others that might not mean anything, but which are interpreted as their detection of your state. And then there is the total paranoia, not the vague uneasiness I just talked about, but the total emotional charge of fear that shoots through one's whole being upon seeing a cop. When one is stoned, one is usually carrying dope, and the thought of getting stopped and arrested is a real and justified fear. It certainly isn't any surprise that heads have a marked tendency to view policemen as the bad guys. Quite often of course, this judgment is simply prejudicial and unfair, preventing any sort of accurate judgment of affairs in a given situation. But that fault exists on both sides of the fence.

With Mary up on the mountain that day, I had my first introduction to grass, to paranoia, to maintaining. When grass is ingested orally, the effects are very physical (depending of course upon dosage) as well as mental. I was very, very stoned that day. We spent a lot of time playing in the snow, watching skiers and trying not to look too suspicious, although a few knowing kids came up to us and said, "You guys are stoned." The ones who could recognize it were drug-users themselves. On our ride home we were completely exhausted. Or to put it another way, we were "crashing." The higher up one goes, the further there is to fall.

It was a relatively short time after that that someone offered to share a joint (a marijuana cigarette) with me. When first starting, smoking marijuana is a mildly painful (physically) experience. The hot smoke has to be drawn into the lungs and held as long as possible. Then the smoke is let out and another "toke" (draw on the joint) is taken. If one smokes too much dope, the throat and lungs become irritated, the result of which may be a cough and sore throat.

During my first year of high school, I probably only turned on a dozen times. And it was always just marijuana or hashish (a concentrated from a grass smoked in a pipe). The main reason was that I didn't have contacts in the dope world with which to acquire grass. It was much harder to get then than it is now. Dope users at that time were a much smaller, more persecuted minority and they were careful about who they sold dope to, knowing that there were "narcs" (kids who give information to the school or police) planted among the students.

When I was first turning on, there was a real significance to turning on. It was an activity engaged in with other people, who, like myself were growth oriented. People who wanted to learn about themselves and others. And the dope was used, at least in part, to that end. Now it is virtually impossible to make generalizations about what sort of persons use dope, there are so many diverse types of people. Sheer numbers prevent rash generalizations. Dope has the knack of opening up new vistas, making things seen that before were hidden. It is, simply, what you make it. It can be shallow if used that way. But it can also be an instrument of exploration and sensitivity. It is a tool and it can either be used or abused. The way I used dope was, I think, very connected with what was happening in my life during the time that I started. For the first time in my life, I was thinking. I was growth-oriented, life-oriented. And when dope came on the scene, I used it as a means to that end. But the danger of dope, one that I fell into a couple of times for brief periods, is of getting lost in the means. Suddenly the means isn't moving towards some end, the means is all there is. When that happened to me, my life began to revolve around dope and I began to get into the drug culture. A culture that is the result of dope at the center of a lot of people's lives.

My heaviest amount of drug use came when I was a junior in high school. I found school an utter bore, but more than that, totally frustrating. It seemed that all channels for creative and original expression were closed by the administration. My thinking had become more and more individual and to the eyes of most, more radical. No longer were the hippies an untouchable mystery. Most of my friends were called hippies. And I began to find myself being fitted into that classification too. I had always been an independent person that never went around with groups of people.

I instinctively dislike the psychology of groups, but I found myself fitting a stereotype and in fact, desiring to be a hippie. The hippie movement is a vast underground network with a strong sense of group identity and part of me wanted the encouragement, the support of that whole network. It was some time later, in fact about a year later that I realized that for me, the compromises I had to make to fit within a standard labelled hippie wasn't worth it. I wasn't living my life purely; being on the outside what I was on the inside.

During that year I would sometimes be stoned for two weeks or a month solid. Smoking dope every day before, during, and after school. It might be at the bus stop, or in a parked car at school, or behind a tree, or in someone's home. The fact that school was for the most part such an unstimulating and oppressive place, made my use of dope during school much more accentuated. If the class wasn't interesting, it was bound to be at least amusing if I went stoned.

As alcohol is the social drug for older generations, grass is (or is rapidly becoming) the social drug for my generation. I know that for a good while, the main reason I was turning on was to make relating easier, to be associated with certain people, to have a good time. One of the reasons kids sometimes have great difficulty giving up dope is that dope is used as a very handy, a very established social aid. Two individuals immediately have something in common if they both turn-on, and if they are both stoned at the same time, that bond becomes even stronger. Dope is used to bring people together.

It was during the times when I was using dope almost exclusively as a social aid that I became quite involved in dope. After being stoned for several days, the reality induced through drugs becomes quite normal and after several weeks, the drug-induced reality becomes the only reality. To quit taking drugs after being stoned several weeks or a month is a trip in itself. Coming down off the drugs, which have accumulated in one's body by this time, is as freaky as going up on them. Once again your reality, your perspective is changed, and you can count on being stoned, without taking any drugs, for another week or so.

It was during my last portion of my junior year that I first dropped LSD or acid, as it is commonly called. The decision to do this was of considerable more personal risk than the decision to try marijuana. Many of my friends and acquaintances had tried it or were deeply imbedded in the world of psychedelics and other hard drugs. I had seen all too clearly how many people had gotten themselves screwed up by taking hard drugs. People who were in mental hospitals, people who couldn't think clearly, even people who were knowingly killing themselves. I knew the extreme dangers and I knew I wouldn't ever let myself get that far. I suppose a lot of people have told themselves that, fooling themselves, but I somehow have a great deal of confidence in myself to pull through and muster up strength when I need it the most. A fear that I had to face when considering experimenting with each drug is the possibility that I might *like* the experience. The possibility existed that I might really like acid, that I might like it so much that I would want to take it again and again and eventually get messed up with it. I am glad that I waited as long as I did before trying acid. By the time I tried it, I had had quite a bit of exposure to the world of psychedelics. I had some idea of the rationalizations and psychological ruts that are an occupational hazard for any heavy doper. I knew what signs to watch for in myself to let me know if things got out of balance.

A major influence in my decision to try acid was knowing and talking to people who had used it and were still very intact. People who knew where to get good, pure acid if I wanted it, who knew what to do and not do when tripping, what kind of situation is best to be in, what kind of people to be around. It's very important to be guided by someone you trust the first several acid trips. So much is happening, so much is coming into your brain that you might lose your ability to keep control and keep it a good experience. I decided to try it.

I found an evening when my parents wouldn't be home and invited some friends over. I had stayed home from school that day. A friend of mine, who had obtained the acid, came over in the afternoon. He pulled out the pill which was very tiny and of a pinkish-purple hue. He sawed it in half with a razor blade and we each swallowed half. It was pure Purple Owsley, which is some of the best and most powerful acid available. It's so hard to get hold of that it is something of a treasure to have some. I remember that sort of horrible, helpless feeling after I swallowed it, knowing that it was in my stomach now and there was nothing I would be able to do about it, but ride it out. We went in to watch T.V. and wait the 45 minutes he said it took for it to take effect.

When I used to ask people in curiosity, what getting stoned on grass or acid was like, they'd smile and say, "Man, there's no way to describe it. It's so different that you have to experience it to understand it." They had a point. To describe an acid trip to someone who hasn't experienced it is almost impossible. No matter how far your imagination will allow you to go, there are regions that are completely beyond your wildest imaginings. And that, in part, is the world of acid. I remember thinking, *feeling* through every pore in my body as I was tripping, "This is more than I ever imagined, ever *could* have imagined! I could never explain this to anyone!"

Colors, in endless streams and patterns emerged from everything I looked at. Sound came roaring through me in waves so that if someone were talking to me, I had to concentrate to understand them. Every sense was more alive than I ever thought possible. For a long time, numbers and letters emerged from every surface in a geometric stampede. My body felt absolutely electric, alive and pulsating in waves of energy. And the music over the stereo seared through me, I was sure leaving burnt holes in my body. It was all so complete. Everything, every perception was totally changed and it didn't last for a few minutes but for ten or twelve hours. I had a very good trip. It was extremely beautiful, happy and free of stress. It is impossible to describe an acid trip because acid is not understood intellectually, it is felt and felt in such an intense degree that you simply must experience it to understand it. The whole early portion of my trip was very sensual, but I had decided before I dropped the acid that I would not allow the trip to be merely sensual, no matter how pleasurable that might be. So after I had peaked (reached the highest point of my trip), I went off by myself in a dark room to think. And that too, was a very good experience. I reviewed my life, some of the relationships with other people I had and I began to have some important insights. Insights, I am well aware, can be as elusive and useless as a mirage.

But these insights were valid and they were of benefit to my life when I was straight (not stoned).

As is often the case, my first acid trip was my best. After I came down I wasn't sure whether I ever wanted to try it again. It was so *unbelievably* powerful. It had been my luck that the power had been used to produce a good, but it was more than a slight possibility that that power would eventually catch me at a bad moment when my head wouldn't be in a good place and I would be off on a bummer that would be as bad as my trip was good.

I did however, try it again. About half a dozen times, but always in small dosages. And for the most part on those occasions it was from fair, to not that good. If I can't justify my use of dope by getting something positive from it, then I stop. And those other times I dropped acid, I didn't enjoy the experiences. It felt so artificial. I think that I basically dislike the sensation of being that stoned. I can remember wanting the trip to stop so I could go back to normal. To top that off, I have a great deal of difficulty maintaining an acid. I react too completely to sensory input. If someone touches me, I jump a mile and I have problems in carrying on any sort of rational conversation with a straight person when I'm stoned. I finally decided that acid wasn't for me.

There are two changes I could have made to make my last half-dozen trips much better. For one thing, I would have taken more acid and on an empty stomach. Naturally, if one has a full stomach, the effects of the drug are diminished. It is an extremely uncomfortable and frustrating experience to be almost, but not quite stoned. Especially with acid. Secondly, I would have picked my environment more carefully. I would have stayed away from hordes of people, or any situation where I'd have to maintain in front of straight people. Maintaining on grass is nothing compared to maintaining on acid. For me, maintaining on acid in front of straight people is practically impossible. I would have, if I had been thinking, tripping on nature. In the woods or at the ocean.

Several things began to happen as a result of my degree of drug use that year. As one uses drugs in quantity, the contacts with the drug-youth culture increases. I began to rub shoulders with dealers, political revolutionaries, addicts, and even with the underworld. The types of people are extremely varied, some are absolute freaks, people who don't hide themselves by fading into normalcy, but who strive to be on the outside what they are on the inside. And sometimes what's inside is very, very different than the norm. I was (and still am for that matter) constantly having my mind blown by people and their life-styles that were totally alien to me. It's an adventure, a challenge, and for me, a necessity to attempt to understand that which is foreign to me. To be able to honestly relate with someone who is very different from me requires sensitivity and openness. And if I am successful in being sensitive, then new vistas are opened.

So drugs and the world that comes with them was for me a vast pool of resources. It can be a positive learning environment. But there is every possible influence within the drug-youth culture. There are those that are negative, say the death trip of speed or heroin and the mental dishonesty and psychological ruts that go along with that. The responsibility is left with the individual to be discerning and make responsible, mature decisions. And there are not a lot of people, young or old, capable of that. The drug culture does not advocate any one line of growth. The strength of the movement is in its openness for diversity of life-styles. There are, however, various circles within the drug culture. Depending on which circle one is involved in, and depending on what hold that circle has on the individual, there is sometimes a great deal of pressure exerted on the individual to conform to group mores, which often includes an exorbitant degree of drug consumption.

It is difficult for me to talk about the drug culture as something completely separate and easily identified and understood. It isn't. It is included, in fact interwoven, in the fabric of the whole youth movement. As a drug user, I had a group of people that were the people I was involved with primarily through drugs. But I also had contact with others within the youth movement who were outside of my little world. Many friends weren't drug users. I think that the diversity and conflict of attitudes was very important. My world wasn't closed to include just drugs and drug users. There were others who were off drugs, who thought that drugs were a bad thing. Interaction with people like that encouraged me to watch myself, to be sensitive to the way I was using drugs.

I think the reason my drug use was in most part, a positive

experience was because I usually attempted to be sensitive to both the positive-negative effects drugs were having on me. There have been times when I have instinctively felt that to take drugs for a given period wouldn't be good. When I sense that, I quit for awhile. That sort of instinctive indicator I call my internal thermostat. It is a certain something within me that sends out warning signals when things are off-balance. And as long as I respond to those warnings, I'm ok. Somehow I thought that everyone had such an indicator within themselves, and I ended up trusting a lot of people and their life styles, only to later find out that they were very out of tune with themselves.

After using drugs quite heavily during a good part of my junior year and getting quite involved, *too* involved in them, I quit turning on for several months. It was during my period of tapering down towards the end of the school year that my mother found some marijuana in my room. Understandably shocked and confused, she made an appointment for me with Dr. Scott, obviously thinking that any child of hers that turned on must be a little mixed up.

I went to my first appointment feeling quite sure of myself and prepared to psych Dr. Scott out. Underneath, however, I was frightened because underneath things weren't all as healthy and strong as they seemed to be on top. And it took him about two minutes to begin touching and exposing the inner confusion and dishonesty. I was verbal and had this image that very few people saw through. Dr. Scott was different. He had few problems in seeing what was beneath. He would ask me a question about an attitude or an idea that I had superficially touched on and he'd allow me to simply make a fool of myself. To trip myself up in my own words. I was mouthing the attitudes of my generation, and when he would begin to ask questions that required a subtle and deep understanding of the topic, I would get lost, simply because those ideas and attitudes weren't my own. I'd just latched onto them. There were contradictions all over the place. In short, I was a bag of hot air. I had this glossy image of myself as mature, intelligent, honest etc. I conceived of myself as having a strong healthy mind. It became very obvious even that first session that all that was a big farce.

I was incapable of anything approaching humility. Humble people are in touch with reality, they have made real decisions. Any form of humility was suspiciously viewed as a threat to my self-image, which was high and unreal. So every time Dr. Scott would do or say something that required a humble or even realistic response, I would fight like mad. One time after trapping me in my own maze of contradictions, he said.

"You're just a scatterbrained blonde, aren't you Jane?"

Every part of me revolted at the idea. It was essential to me to keep the image intact, irregardless of whether it was right or wrong.

Silence, I was extremely tense and nervous. I always was at our sessions. I felt threatened, on the defensive.

"Jane, won't you agree that you're just a 16-year-old scatterbrained blonde?"

"I wouldn't say I was scatterbrained. At least not all the time" I said tentatively, trying to avoid being a braggart, a role he could crush easily. I was trying to appease him. Trying to compromise. Attempting to get him off my back.

"Oh. So you're scatterbrained just *some* of the time?" He was smiling at me. I remember so well that horrible feeling of being trapped. For me to argue the point would have made me talk like a fool. I would be boasting and both of us would see through that. I could feel the phoniness, but it was essential to my image to not give in. I wouldn't let myself see it too clearly. He kept on pressing me. "Jane, say, 'I am a scatterbrained blonde.' "

"No!" I exclaimed in terror.

"Come on Jane. You can do it. It isn't hard. 'I am a scatterbrained blonde.' "

Silence. I was trapped. Why should it be so hard for me to be a little humble? Because it's too hard to be real. I didn't want to be real. I wasn't a real person.

"That's too honest Dr. Scott."

"Say it."

"I am a scatterbrained blonde." I whispered it.

"I couldn't hear you Jane. Could you speak up a little more? Say it like you *mean* it."

Why couldn't he leave good enough alone? Not only to have to say it, but to say it with emphasis, with feeling. "I am a scatterbrained blonde." I said it. It was out. I was through and it felt good.

"Good. That wasn't so bad was it?"

My six months with Dr. Scott was very good for me. My thinking was screwy. I began to see the gigantic difference between the Jane of words, books and images and the Jane, the real Jane, underneath. It was by his constantly forcing the two worlds to face each other that I realized how phony I really was. I began to have some sense of what was real and what wasn't and that knowledge allowed me to develop some sense of inner direction. A certain degree of inner honesty began to emerge. I was beginning to get in contact with myself. I was shocked that I had allowed myself to grow as out of contact with myself as I had. The drugs and the drug culture had affected me more superficially than I had realized. I had allowed most of my new input to feed the image, but it never touched the frightened, lonely, vulnerable Jane that was underneath. I had used the culture to make myself invulnerable, I had used it to keep up the image. It became clear, through my session with Dr. Scott, that I was using the group identity of the hippies to hide from myself.

The group identity was not, is not, my identity. And that is a fantastically important distinction. Suddenly I was having to deal with myself for the first time in my life. Being answerable to myself and not the group. I suppose I'm giving the impression that I was some sort of hard core hippie. I wasn't. There were however, certain psychological ties that I was responding to. My case wasn't particularly extreme, but it was dangerous for me as an individual because it was allowing me to be out of touch with myself. I began to see some of the phoniness in certain other people in the way they followed the group, not really dealing with themselves. My whole perspective had changed. I was able to view my reality much more objectively.

As I think back over that time, I realize that my experience with Dr. Scott was a major turning point for me. If I had gone on in the direction I was heading, I might have gotten really messed up in a lot of different things. I began to understand what inner honesty meant and what it entailed. And as a result, I was gaining a more realistic conception of myself. In short, Dr. Scott helped me clean out some of the rubbish and equipped me with some of the raw tools to aid me in continuing to clean out the garbage and grow in a positive healthy direction.

I don't want to give the impression that dope was the cause of my psychological imbalance. The problems Dr. Scott and I worked on were things that had developed out of my not dealing with my reality constructively before I ever started turning on. I used my reality, which at that time was drugs and the drug culture, simply as the externals with which to rationalize and cover up the internal.

By the time Dr. Scott had gotten me on my feet and I was no longer a patient of his, I was well into my senior year of high school. I was using drugs off and on in moderate quantities, depending on where my head was at. For quite a while, I was involved in meditation, as I happen to be right now. And during this time, I couldn't turn on because meditation and dope are instrinsically incompatible. During another period of abstinence, I was on a health kick, attempting to purify my body.

One major factor that tends to influence when and to what degree I use dope is the type of people I am with when turning on. Presently there are very few people that I think use dope positively, as a learning growing experience. Getting stoned with most people I know feels like a regression to times gone by for me. The more I grow, the fewer people I like to get stoned with. Perhaps eventually there will be no one, and if that happens, then my use of drugs will draw to a final close.

I had various experiences with other drugs, including T.H.C., speed, opium, cocaine, and mescaline. Different drugs of course produce different stones. And different people respond to and enjoy different sorts of stones depending on what kind of person they happen to be.

Grass is nice for everyday use, or rather, one can maintain and function in one's reality and still be stoned and hence enjoy the whole experience. It is relatively mild and non-incompacitating. The reality of a drug can become very boring too, when it becomes as commonplace and frequent (or more frequent) than contacts with the "real" world. I simply have tired of the world of marijuana. I know it too well and at this point it isn't opening new vistas as it once did, but simply revisiting old ones.

Grass is mild and pleasant, opium is powerful and positively euphoric. I really enjoyed opium. In mild doses, it produced a state of a deep, thoughtful and rich euphoria. I could maintain. I didn't lose my power to think rationally and in fact it produced a state where I was induced to quietly and happily pursue my thoughts. Thinking became a sort of sensuous experience. Grass often tends to make everything fragmented, but opium makes everything flow together. But knowing that opium is expensive, relatively hard to get, and addicting kept me from pursuing my interest.

I am a person that doesn't like to be incompacitated by a drug. Some people do. I definitely do not like to have my powers of thinking seriously impaired while stoned. I tend therefore, to not take dope in very large dosages, and to take those drugs which leave me in some sort of contact with myself and the world. Acid and mescaline were simply too much. Too alien, too artificial for me. Mescaline is not nearly as distorting as acid and because of this it is used more widely than acid.

One very definite occupational hazard of doping and particularly dropping is the threat of bad, contaminated dope. Acid often has strychnine in it which among other things produces headaches and muscle cramps. Strychnine accumulates in the body and if one takes enough bad acid it can build to such a degree that heart failure occurs. Speed is also often added to acid and mescaline. It is amazing to me how indiscriminate some people are in getting their dope. Some people simply want to be high all the time and don't really care how its done and what is sacrificed. But not all dope is contaminated. If one is careful and concerned about the quality of dope, there are dealers that are reputable and can obtain good stuff. I also know of people who have their pills chemically tested to make sure of their purity.

It isn't too hard for me to understand how people can get very involved in speed. Speed makes one feel very, very alive. In moderate quantities one is completely rational, but the process of reacting and thinking is speeded up. Fantastically lengthy and deep conversations are bound to happen while speeding with someone else. In fact, it's hard to shut up when speeding. Its an incredibly fast experience, and as sometimes happens with fast things, one begins saying, "Faster, faster!" When that happens and the urge is succombed to, the possibility of entrenchment in the world of speed becomes a very real threat. In greater doses, powers of thinking and functioning are very definitely impaired. Needless to say, there are all kinds of speed, from caffeine to Dexedrine to Methedrine®. I enjoy the experience of thinking rapidly and productively, not sleeping or eating in a splurge of activity. But all drugs involve a process of crashing, and coming off speed is particularly uncomfortable. In fact, I hate it. My body reacts very sensitively to all forms of dope. If after taking, say, just one tab (tablet) of Dexedrine, a mild sort of speed, I feel abnormal and off-balance for about three or four days. Not to mention one full day of crashing. I intensely dislike not being all here when I want to be. Because of this and because when one gets into speed it's very easy to become entrenched in it, I don't use it any more.

A lot of what happens when one is stoned is contingent on how one has learned to use dope. Doping is in large part a learned behavior. Often when someone tries grass just once or twice, not much happens. This is partly because a beginner doesn't know how to draw in and hold in the smoke. But it is also partly because the beginner hasn't learned to pick up on things. For instance, listening to music is a sure shot. Dope intensifies everything. One's ability to get deeply involved in the music is greatly enhanced. Music is extremely important to my generation. It isn't simply a form of casual entertainment. Music portrays all of the major forces in existences within the youth movement and indeed all those forces perceived to be a part of society and *life* (in the spiritual sense). Music is a mental, physical, spiritual-exploration, and discovery.

Everyone has their own pattern of perceiving reality and that pattern has the opportunity to change when stoned. Some people are in just one giant body trip. They react to everything purely sensually. It's simply one sensation rolling in after the other. There are others that make doping a mental exercise, postulating over all the possible subtleties and their various implications; and there are those that attempt to use it as a method of spiritual exploration.

And of course, there are all varying degrees of combinations of these.

The way that one uses dope depends to a large degree on the group one is with. The fact that my friends tended to be strong, individualistic, growth-oriented people, I know made a great deal of difference in the way I learned to use dope and the attitude I developed towards it. An individual tends to use drugs in the way that his peers do. When dope comprises 50 to 75 to 100% of a person's life (which is not uncommon), the ramifacations of peer group control become very striking.

I can't stand back and say that dope was entirely bad or good for me. It was both good and bad. On a few occasions I got lost in the world of dope. And it was easy for me while doping to be satisfied with insights and no action. The fact that for awhile I identified with a group ideal meant that for awhile I was short-changing myself as an individual. I was also thrown in with certain individuals whom I was very vulnerable to and whom affected me negatively. But growing means taking risks, and it means having failures and making mistakes.

Through drugs, unexplored regions of my mind were opened to me. Perhaps I didn't really discover much in the way of substance, but I at least gained an appreciation of the fact that there are vast unexplored realms and levels of consciousness that are possible, as yet unexplored and undeveloped, but still possible. I was slowly drawn into a world that consisted of vast and rich resources. Art, music, philosophy, spiritualism and much more are all available. Drugs and the culture surrounding them opened new doors for me. Doors which opened up on new and exciting horizons.

Chapter VI

TWO YEARS EXPERIENCE HELPING TEEN-AGED DRUG ABUSERS

Chuck Paulus

M Y two years experience of working with teen-aged drug abusers and their families have been the most rewarding experience of my life. At this time, I want to express a note of thanks for those who made this opportunity possible; first, to the State of Oregon Mental Health Division, and Mr. George Dimas, director of the Alcohol and Drug Section; and second, to Dr. Edward M. Scott and his staff at the Treatment and Training Center.

During the two years of work with young drug users I saw nearly two hundred drug users. These young people ranged in age from 12 to 18, and their drug use ran through all the typical drugs —LSD, peyote, marijuana, etc. Most of them dressed in the "hippie-style" though there were a few exceptions. Hence, most wore long hair, had patches on their jeans, etc. The majority came from white middle class homes in the Portland metropolitan area.

Perhaps, it would be a safe generalization to say that most of the teen-aged drug abusers with whom I worked were sensitive, searching for answers, and questioned the values of their parents.

Initially, most of them were shy and somewhat suspicious of me, and all had to test me by a variety of gambits. Once they felt I could be trusted, they would pour their hearts out to me and develop a lasting loyalty. I have never known one to lie to me or let me down — if he stayed in the program for at least six months. This, I think, is a crucial finding.

I have made numerous home visits, and typically when the parents learn that their child is using drugs, there is complete dismay. I have known some parents who were unaware of their child's drug use for a period of 2½ years. Other parents have

81

punished their children, search their child's personal property, listen in on phone calls, and check for typical signs without learning about the drug abuse. In a few instances, similar parental behavior has *caused* their child to turn to drugs — the constant accusations have finally convinced the teen-ager to say "why not? I'm accused of it anyway."

It is usually the mother who is first suspicious, and her initial reaction to her own suspicion, is to doubt it. One mother requested her 15-year-old daughter to say, "Tell me it isn't so!" When the daughter replied, "Yes, mother, I have used drugs," it nearly overwhelmed the mother.

Most often when the father learns of his child's drug use, he remains calm, attempting to find out the source of the drugs. When the "third degree" fails, he often threatens, and imposes unrealistic restrictions. During this confrontation, mother cries, asking, "Where did we go wrong?"

Some frantic parents, ask their child to leave their home at once; others call the police, while still other parents, seemingly give a kind of "permission" to continue using drugs, by relaxing rules, increase of allowance, etc.

It is my estimation that on the whole, the parents are conscientious, concerned, hard working, charitable people according to their standards. They try to live by the codes established by the majority in their social circle. They want the best for their children, and work to provide opportunities.

In spite of the good will and concern, there are certain ingredients which are lacking. I want to mention a few of these. Many parents believe the only problem is that of drug abuse. I don't see it this way. There are other issues which are more formidable hurdles — lack of plans for the future, changing values, an almost "about face" of everything taught by the parents.

Also, I am rather certain that most often the teen-agers complain in order to justify their use of drugs. During one of my home visits, the following remarks were made by a teen-ager,

> Marijuana is less harmful than alcohol. All my friends use it. I know it is illegal, but so is drinking for minors. You said you did that when you were young. You just don't understand. I love you as my parents, but you talk at me. You pick my friends for me and plan my future. If I don't fit into your mold, you're hurt and disappointed.

You don't give me direct, honest answers to many of my questions; so I've gone to my peers and now you say, what I've learned is bad.

You have been so busy making money, building this beautiful home, providing me with the best, but too busy to give me love and affection. You're not happy. I've never seen you even kiss mom. She works hard to please you. She spends all day cleaning and rearranging the furniture. You come home and say, "Where is my chair?" You sit down to a meal, she's worked at creating and you never even say a thank you.

And mom, dad comes home tired and worn out and you never ask him about his day. I never see you touch him.

Perhaps, I should relate something about the condition in which many of the teen-aged drug abusers come to the clinic. Let's take the example of Jim (let's call him). He was a 17-year-old boy. When I asked if I could help him, he just stared at me. I assured him I wanted to help him. He hesitated, then blurted out, "I am going crazy and need help." For the next hour I listened and that is all I did. He came from a middle class family. His father was an executive in a large corporation. His mother spent most of her time socializing and going to church. There was a younger sister who hated him and was idolized by his parents. Since he was 12, he had spent periods of time living with his grandparents and an aunt.

At the age of 12, he began to use drugs starting with glue sniffing. At the peak of his glue sniffing it took as much as 10 tubes of model airplane glue to get him "high." When he was 14 he started to use marijuana and at 15 he had tried LSD. When he was 16 he went to California and lived with a family who belonged to Hell's Angels. He had not used drugs for 3 months, but was having flashbacks.

The clinic staff decided to place him in group therapy, and I was to see him individually; and to make home visits. Jim had related to me that his family was not a close family. I must say the family did have some rather unconventional rules. They never gathered as a family, aside from the evening meal. There was a rule — no one talks at dinner. After dinner, the father retired to his quarters which consisted of a living room, bedroom and bath; and the mother to her quarters, which was the same, and the two children to each of their own rooms.

The evening I visited, we met in the family living room. I had the eerie feeling that we were all strangers. Conversation was strained and difficult. In spite of several months of attempting to help this family, I was rather unsuccessful; although, in a way some success did ensue.

Jim was able to remain off drugs for a year, but as troubles returned, he resorted to drug use again and is now back at the clinic.

Group therapy is a treatment technique utilized for all the drug users. Generally, the first month or two is rather nonproductive, with little movement or behavior change appearing. Gradually, changes in their facial features appear. They seem happier, smiling, talkative, and looking forward to the next day. Their attitudes seem to show improvement. They speak with more respect, for their parents, for school, and even for the *establishment*. In the group, they begin to have courage to take an individualistic stand. For instance, a girl said during group therapy, "I am sick and tired of playing your game of being against everything. I know there needs to be change in society. I left home for two months and found out it wasn't all a bed of roses, which I thought it would be. When I returned home, my mother said, "I love you and want you to live here." I told her how much I loved her and needed her. I found out I needed people who really loved me. There are two ways of playing the game; just taking, or by giving."

Another significant change is their attempt to understand things they do not like — instead of fighting against it, or belittling what they do not understand.

On a reality level, significant changes begin to emerge — their grades begin to improve. Some have made impressive improvement; grades changing from F and "incompletes" to A, B, and C's.

There is, additionally, confirmatory evidence as I learn from my home visits. One parent stated, "I am so happy for what has happened to my child. Oh, she still smokes a little grass, and runs around with those long-haired friends with the patches on their jeans, long skirts, and no shoes, what I really like is that we can talk, and the family is a unit — again." Another member stated, "My parents are great. I used to think they were changing, but now I am not sure that they changed at all. I guess I just understand them better."

A teen-aged boy said, "When we first started this group, I came to get support for my negative attitude toward life. We were all against the adult society, and what it stood for. Now I come to find the answers to some problems that I alone cannot handle. This group has taught me to love myself."

Often the home visits, at which parents and their teen-agers were both present, afforded an excellent opportunity for bargaining. One mother, was willing to concede on many points but not on the matter of long hair for her teen-aged son. After some weeks of discussion, a compromise was reached — he could grow his hair to " . . . just below the ears." Several weeks later this same mother while listening to a parent complain about their daughter's use of drugs stated, "You make me sick — the problem with you is that you can't see through the marijuana smoke and under the long hair to find a beautiful, lovely daughter who needs you."

It has been repeatedly gratifying to observe how parents and teen-agers can relate, bargain, understand, and love each other. Permit me to relate an incident of this type. During one of my home visits, a mother related an experience which changed the relationship between herself and her 15-year-old daughter — an experience in which both were open and honest. Following this honest exchange, the mother reported, "I forget about her drug abuse and become concerned about her problem and feelings." The daughter said, "I don't need drugs, mom turns me on."

As the teen-agers improve, and leave the group they take great care to express their thanks. I have received many, very flattering comments. One teen-ager wrote the following letter.

Dear Mr. Paulus:

I've been trying to think of a way to thank you for all the help and support you have given me. So I'll just remember back over the time I've known you. The first time I met you, I was scared. You seemed so straight and potentially mean. I didn't trust you at all. After the war of silence, I began to talk and to listen, and listening really hurt. People are always picking at my best hidden secrets. It was nice to see you worry; it went clear through my icy, cold sheet.

I remember all the work it took to build a trust and now that it's so solid I can't let it go. Can you? You helped me grow past the stage of isolation. I learned from you to put into practice *caring for others*. I found a path to follow. It is to be close to true friends, and the farther along this path I go, the more distant seem the dope freaks and self-destroying people of my past.

Now I've a life, something to work for and people to share things with — and Mr. Paulus — please stay the way you are, relaxed and confident. But please stay tough when it is needed. People need love and friendship, but they also need some kind of responsibility and Mr. Paulus, you showed me mine. Keep on showing people theirs. I remember you always got mad when we complained about something, you tried to make us change it, not just complain. I'm sorry, this letter has to end, I'm crying . . ."

Thanks,
Sue

Expressions of appreciation are received from many parents. A father expressed himself by saying,

> The group therapy that our daughter has received has changed her outlook and her ability to cope with problems that at one time seemed so insurmountable to her. I sincerely feel that your guidance will help her to grow into a normal productive adult. I wish to extend my appreciation for the counseling that my wife and I received and the group therapy for parents. To say the least, it saved our daughter from being the product of another broken home. It is very difficult for people our age to understand the younger generation without being polarized. In our case, you acted as a catalyst and I am convinced that if it were not for group therapy and home visits, our situation would have worsened.

Thanks,
Mr. Jones

It is my impression that most, if not all, teens who use drugs of any kind do so by choice and not by necessity, and the drug abuser is a specialist in knowing this, but he will attempt, time and again to justify his drug abuse. The young people with whom I worked, know a tremendous amount about drugs, more than their parents.

It is my opinion that drug abuse is frequently associated with problems other than drugs. Laws, jails, punishment, educational programs and clinics are important, but not the key factor. I believe the key factor in all of our efforts to understand and help the young drug user is to substitute reason for fear. Secondly, the parents play an important role in which they mingle the proper amounts of love and discipline. If the teen-ager has not experienced reasonable discipline in the home (which is a form of love) they often give a kind of uncontrolled response to the seeking of gratification in drugs.

Regarding results, the following aspects reflect impressions gained during my two years of working with teen-aged drug dependent persons.

In the discussion of results, a division will be made, which hopefully will help the reader to better understand my assessment of the parameters.

I. Drugs
   1. About 10% have stopped using *all* illicit drugs.
   2. About 50% of those who have stopped using "hard" or hallucinogens, still use marijuana, occasionally. Their parents are aware of this, and would rather they did not use marijuana, even occasionally, but feel that the overall results are sufficient to tolerate this.
   3. Hence, for those attending group therapy, there is improvement in 60%, regarding the use of drugs.
   4. The remainder (40%) have failed to continue either at the clinic, or attend family groups (which takes place in homes).

II. Other Reality Factors
   1. Improvement is not merely limited to the drug usage. The real changes have taken place in their attitudes, behavior, communication with parents, and school attendance. They are no longer isolating themselves from the society in which they live — rather they have become part of it.

III. New Modalities
   1. A special type of "project" deserves to be reported. One group of drug users, who lived in one neighborhood, and were well acquainted, met with their parents (weekly) in different homes. The group of parents and teens developed a loyalty and quickly "see-to-it," if one of the group failed to make a session.
   2. This group, totaled twenty-two teen-aged drug users, plus their parents. From that total number, thirteen stopped using drugs, attended school, and could bargain with their parents.

3. Those who still used drugs, drifted away, making new friends.
4. Five of the thirteen will graduate from high school this year. All were accepted into college; three graduated last year, and are now in college.
5. Five and a half years ago, none had wanted to attend classes in high school and were "chronic skippers."
6. This "neighborhood experiment" has more potential for success than the typical settings. If parents and teens will accept some initial guidance from a trained worker, and allow the problem to emerge, the rate of success, I think, cannot only be duplicated, but bettered.

IV. Community Action

1. In addition to therapeutic activity for themselves and the families, some of the teen-agers have participated actively in numerous educational programs for the community.
2. For the past year and a half, I have used 12 young drug abusers (most are *former* drug abusers) in the following community educational activities.
   a. High school, PTA, and teacher education workshops.
   b. Private civic groups: Kiwanis, Lions, JayCees, and other such groups.
   c. Private industry — Northwest Bell
   d. Television

In one month alone, these 12 teen-agers talked to over 8 thousand people in the State of Oregon.

The method of presenting a program varies with special interests of the group requesting our program, but we do have "a standard method" of presentation. This method emerged as a result of several trial and error sessions.

3. Typically, the following method is utilized.
   a. I have a brief interview with each teen-ager on the panel. This interview revolves around their introduction to drugs, the effects of the drugs, and the concerns.
   Our aim is to say just enough to get the audience thinking and desirous of learning more about drugs.

    b. At the point in which I feel this desire is "ready," we turn it over to the audience to ask questions. The reaction of most audiences has been positive, with an occasional criticism.

    c. After the performance, the teen-agers have been treated by: hugging, "cried over," praise, and understanding. They have received invitations to dinners, invited to weekends, and to go on picnics by numerous adults from the audience.

4. Perhaps the most effective programs have been done as a series of the following steps.

    a. On the first presentation, a panel of drug abusers, as indicated above.

    b. On the second presentation, parents of drug abusers.

    c. A third phase is the combination of young drug abusers and parents — but NOT the parents of the members of the panel.

This third phase is a real learning experience for the panelists (adults and teen-agers) as it is for the audience. It is my feeling that those present "catch" this and benefit accordingly.

Following this type of program, the audience often states reactions such as the following.

    a. "Drugs aren't the main problem, the real problem is people."

    b. Adults realize that younger people are struggling with problems, not really trying to avoid them.

    c. Teen-agers appreciate adults, "Gosh, I feel ashamed for the way I have talked about older generation," and, "These people treated me great."

    d. A few adults will privately approach some of our teen panelists and quietly say, "I've used marijuana and liked it better than alcohol."

    e. A small percentage of the audience are critical, concerned about legal matters, and about cutting off the source of supply.

5. A third method of presentation is utilizing a panel of drug abusers and non-drug users on the same panel. At times the audience is polarized, and at times the panelists

are polarized. Then again, the differences which emerge seem minimal.

We have kept a record of the number of people our teen-aged drug abusers have talked to. In one year and a half 30,000 people (young, old, adults, teachers, parents, lawyers, and professional therapists) have heard us. We hope we have "reached" many of our listeners. The response suggests that we have.

Saslow (1970) notes that one manner of preventing drug abuse is to participate in the social aspects of one's community. If Saslow's notion is valid, our panelists are really in the process of rehabilitation.

I have found my work to be "addictive," I hope to continue in it for the rest of my life.

Chapter VII

A DIALOGUE BETWEEN DRUG USING AND NON-DRUG USING TEEN-AGERS

IN numerous therapy sessions, both in group and individual sessions, drug using teen-agers made reference to the fact that they did not talk, or relate to non-drug using peers at times, they make sarcastic references to "squares," "honest Johns," etc.

When I suggested at one of their group therapy sessions that they have a meeting with their non-drug using peers, I met with some initial resistance. This resistance was rather quickly resolved by some of the members who pointed out that it would be an opportunity to try and understand one another. Since lack of understanding was often a topic of discussion, it was felt that this might be an opportunity to be understood and to understand.

I made the arrangements for the meeting to be held at my office.

The drug using teens were patients of mine at the clinic, and, therefore, represent, to a degree, individuals who are attempting to solve some of their problems.

The non-drug using teens are typical individuals attending public high schools in the Portland Metropolitan area.

A tape recorder was operating during the session, and the following dialogue is taken verbatim from part of the session.

I have changed the names of the participants. It will be helpful for the reader to recognize the following "team members."

Non-Drug Using Teens	*Drug Using Teens*
Tom	Bill
Sue	Joe
Dick	Kathy
Mary	Betty

The participants were introduced to each other, and each teen-ager gave a quick summary of his family, of himself, and his opinion on drugs.

Once this type of formality was completed, the dialogue began.

Tom: I want to know why you took drugs in the first place.

Joe: I am still working on that problem. I just tried it at first. I started popping tranquilizers, sleeping pills, barbiturates, as people call them, and the only reason I did was a couple friends said, "Hey man, you ought to try some of these, they are just like drinking a couple cases of beer." My mother was taking them for multiple sclerosis, so I had quite a quantity of them. She would take one of them and I would be taking 4 of them. A week of her prescription would last about one day.

Tom: Why do you take drugs? Was it just because someone talked you into it, or did you want to find yourself?

Betty: Well, for most of my life I have heard my dad say, "Look at marijuana, if you take it, you are going to be on it for the rest of your life and you will be addicted." I could not believe it because he is sitting there taking his pills to get up and pills to go to sleep. So I finally decided to try it and I really liked it.

Dick: Why did you like it?

Kathy: Well, people use things for escape.

Tom: Why couldn't you find a reality in reality? Why did you have to see beauty where it isn't a real beauty? It seems that if one just sits and thinks, he can see beauty and if they want they can escape within themselves. Why did you wish to escape through drugs to find whatever you were looking for?

Kathy: Well, whenever you are using drugs everything is real. Everything is a reality.

Sue: Do you think drugs are a reality? It seems they are an escape from reality, something supernatural.

Kathy: What is real to you when you are on drugs you realize that it doesn't really matter whether it really exists to other people. It's like your own surroundings. If you are up on a trip, you are experiencing something no one else can see, and it doesn't really bother you because you're doing your own thing.

Dick: When you come back off a trip or any kind of drugs, do you say to yourself, "I wish I had never gone on that trip, why am I using these?"

Kathy: You don't say that when you come off as much as you say that occasionally when you are on. I always seem to come up with a reason not to use drugs when I was on something, but as soon as I was off it, I would forget what it was.

Tom: You said you took drugs because you wanted to escape and so you found this out and this is why then that you kept taking them because you wanted this, your so-called reality in drugs all the time, but how can it really be real if you are dependent on something to find reality?

Betty: Everybody finds reality through something else. A lot of people use religion for reality, and I couldn't under religion, so I turned to drugs.

Sue: I understand that you are now off drugs, what made you decide to come off them?

Kathy: I decided to drop drugs a number of times, and like I said before, I would always find a good reason when I was on something for not using drugs, and then I would get on a bad trip or something and really see the pointlessness of taking drugs and stay off them for a while and it would get to the point where I thought I would enjoy them again. I had a religious conversion myself and that wasn't necessarily the main reason for my stopping drugs, because I don't feel that it had a great deal to do with it because I still had to find out whether I felt drugs were right or wrong. A friend of mine died of an overdose. Other things were happening, some of my friends were going insane.

Mary: Doesn't it sort of bother you at times that it might hurt your parents that you take drugs?

Joe: Yes, but my parents do take drugs. Most parents do, they take pills to get up and go to sleep on and they use the same drugs they are telling you not to use.

When I got busted I thought my old man was going to disown me for good, but he didn't, he said, "You are still my son, there is not much I can do about that, I still like you as my son." I never realized I could hurt him that much, but he expected I would before I ever even did. He saw it in me I guess — my mother started out taking pills every morning, she ended up as a pill fiend. I never worried that much about it hurting my dad. Maybe he has been too good to me, he has always given me complete freedom of myself and it has been up to me to decide what to do. He says, "You will pay for it. It won't hurt me, I might take some harrassment for it, but you are the one who is going to have to live with yourself for another 50 years."

Dick: You said reality now is just useless. In the world all over there is always some wrong, there is always something that is going to hurt, but why look for these things because even when you are escaping through your drugs there are the bad trips, the wrong and the hurt, so why not face the good in the reality we have? Are you happy, are you really satisfied with what you are, of what you are doing. Can you say, "I know what I am going to be and I am happy about what I am?"

Joe: Yes, I really am happy, thanks to drugs. I can give drugs one credit, for my getting busted. I was kicked out of school several times even before I took drugs, or having to stay after school for something. Recently I was completely kicked out of school, and now I am assistant auto mechanic technician and I am making two dollars and twenty-five cents an hour just fixing cars. I am happy with myself. I have stayed off needles because I went to Dr. Scott's clinic, I was using the needle before that. I am still using drugs, but not using the same things I was using. I use weed and things once in a while. If I want to go out on the weekend, either I am going to get drunk or stoned. I would rather get stoned, because then I don't have a hangover and it is all over in 4 hours, but if I drink it is 8 hours of misery after.

Tom: My definition of reality is seeing both the good and the bad. I believe there is a lot more bad than there is good, but being a well-rounded individual means that you can look at both of these and adjust to both of them and still be able to use defense mechanisms to soak it into you, but not let it come so far in that it warps the personality and if you are able to accept things you can see beauty in nature or you can see beauty in people or you can be satisfied, you can be actually happy even though you know there are many bad things in this world that need to be corrected, and drugs is an escape, I feel, so that you do not have to cope with these problems. You do not have to find an answer to them.

Sue: You think drugs are a crime, doesn't this bother you?

Joe: Not really, because of all the times I have been busted I think I am a 4-time loser in the Narcotics Bureau. The longest time I ever did was 60 days for it, and 60 days isn't that much time. The crime part of it never bothered me. Three of those times, charges were dropped. This last time they did stick me with two felonies. Felonies don't really bother me because they are talking now of reforming the drug laws. They are going to have to, because it is ruining a lot of peoples' lives. Another point nobody has ever looked at, who makes these drugs, who makes the barbiturates and amphetamines. We surely don't. It is the pharmacists, most of the speed that is going around is pharmaceutically processed.

Sue: You are right, they do, but they don't make them for you to use, they are for a purpose.

Joe: People who distribute them like pharmacists sell them to your mothers and fathers and we get ahold of them through there. Drugs aren't tight, I can go into a store and buy a bunch of Contacs® and separate the speed from them because I know which little particles it is because I used to do it.

Betty: For what reason do you feel that it should bother a person that it is against the law to take drugs, do you think that they are afraid of being punished.

Sue: No, it is not that they are afraid of being punished, if I were to take drugs, it would be on my conscience for the rest of my life, and that would bother me.

Joe: Do you think that the actually taking of drugs themselves is evil, or do you think that the fact that you broke the law would plague you for the rest of your life?

Sue: Well, breaking the law, that is not good. There is a reason for laws. I would feel bad, it would be on my conscience I wouldn't be able to stand it.

Joe: That's odd. I have never been able to see that. Just because something is a law I couldn't say that that was a reason for me to obey it. It didn't bother my conscience, I might be afraid of being caught.

Sue: There is no law that you can't lie to your parents, but if I ever lied to my parents that would bother me.

Joe: What is the difference. In the case of lying to your parents, you feel that is wrong don't you? What I am saying is that the reason you would not use drugs is not that it is against the law, but because you feel it is wrong. That is what would bother your conscience right?

Tom: Well, part of it is that if you can break the law, you can't get a job with the Federal government and things like that.

Joe: Did it only bother you because of consequences, because you feel like you would be punished, you would feel some ill effects from your action or just because it is wrong?

Tom: Just because it is wrong. It would bother me.

Joe: That is what I was getting at. You were trying to get him to say doesn't it bother you that it is against the law, and yet you actually are saying yourself that the reason it bothers you is not because it is against the law, but because you feel it is wrong.

Tom: Well, it is against the law because it is wrong.

Joe: It doesn't bother me law-wise, the law is the law and I can't change the law. Maybe some day I will be able to — with two felonies against me I guess I am supposed to lose my right to vote, old civic service — I can't go around being governor or senator, it's a bad thing in your campaign you know. That's stupid, if you are going to judge someone on his past, his past isn't going to do anything to the present. When I am 30 I don't want to be judged on what I was when I was 15.

Mary: Do you guys feel drugs themselves are wrong?

Bill: No. well that's avoiding the question. You see, I don't really know. I don't want to try to make any judgments. Whether taking the pill and being stoned is wrong, whether doing something that is enjoyable is wrong, well, I don't want to worry about it. The only thing I would worry about is the effect. Like the adults who don't worry about what's this doing to the kids, it seemed to me they were bugged because we were doing something that was fun — they were worrying about the wrong things. Lots of people don't like to see other people happy.

Mary: Maybe the parents of kids who take drugs don't really feel like that. Maybe — we had talked about reality and he said he thought it was being able to look at our world objectively, having a completely open mind and being able to make the good grow in ourselves and understand the bad. Maybe the parents think "my child isn't fulfilling himself, using all of his ability." So perhaps they are just really hurt and sad.

Bill: When I was talking about older people, I wasn't talking about parents because my parents never knew I was taking drugs. Their main hassle was with my hair. They never knew too much about what was going on.

Mary: What did you say to them when they talked about your hair — I'm just curious.

Bill: All through high school I kept it cut short. There was nothing I could do about it — I had to live at home and so I did pretty much what my parents told me to do. There were two things I couldn't accept and I finally had to break the ties with my family after I had started to college. First was the hair cut — they could not compromise; and second, I couldn't play any rock and roll which was what I had been working towards since my first year in high school, so I decided to leave, which I did.

Sue: Do you people think that maybe parents are partly the cause of a child taking drugs? We young adults of today must find our identity and we need our independence. We have to be responsible and make our own heterosexual decisions and our vocational decisions. We have to be helped and guided by our parents, they can't hang on to us and we can't be dependant upon them, so I wonder, Joe, if you were dependant upon your parents or if they didn't trust or let you make up your mind. They didn't let you make up your mind about the band thing; so it is so important that our parents let us find ourselves, let us know who we are, give us our independence, be responsible — trust us. So, do you think parents are maybe partly the cause?

Bill: I don't really blame my parents for any of my problems. For one thing, the reason they didn't want me to get into a band was that they said I would get in with all those musicians and end up taking drugs and doing all those things. They weren't really so wrong, but the funny thing is if they had let me get into a band, I would probably have gotten sick of it when I was about a junior in high school and given up on the idea, but because I never got to do it, it was something I felt I had to do because I had never done it. Like, it was a cool thing. I actually kind of had to do it before I could feel it wasn't an answer for everything.

I think a big factor is society and our parents are a part of the present society. In my family there were certain — well, I have been loved and I knew I was loved and I loved my parents. Up until the age of about 12, they made all the decisions. Oh, I made small ones like I could wear my tennis shoes or my sandals to the game but I could not make any decisions — big ones. Once I reached the teen-age level, I was making most of the decisions. Now, if my parents had said "these things you can do and these things you can't do," I would have said, "gee, I can't smoke — so, I'm going to smoke, and I can't drink — so I'm going to drink." These are big things that happen sometimes. Because of the rules against them, lots of kids do them. Because there were no rules that said I couldn't do it, like my parents said, "If you want to do it, we can't really stop you." I tried smoking — I puffed the first one to prove I was a man and so twenty years for now I quit to prove the same thing, and if I don't in 50 years I will maybe die of cancer. I look at it as what good will it do me. Does it help me? If it won't help, I won't do it — I can do enough wrong things without trying to think up some more. So, I feel with parents like mine who give me a choice, I usually make up my mind the right way, at least the way society thinks is right.

You are talking in terms of being sensible as though you are alright and have things under control and can make decisions, but when you reach the point where you don't care about the long run or even the short run that much. I don't know what kind of feelings you have experienced along the lines of absolute depression when actually nothing matters to you any more. People can't get the idea that sometimes a person who takes drugs takes them just because they have never had the experience and when they take them they find they can't make a decision and they act irrational.

Sue: Are you trying to say that, for instance, if my mother died and that made me feel depressed . . .

Bill: I don't know how you would feel if your mother died, but suppose you reach a point where you actually didn't care about anything, anything could happen and it wouldn't make you happy — nothing would make you happy. In a case like this you would see where all of a sudden the sensation of drugs is like going into a new world and it is appealing.

Tom: Yes but why did you come from a normal level so far down? There has to be a reason. I think the ability of a well-rounded person — I hate that word — don't like normal either — is able to come from the bottom up to a level without using some other method.

Betty: How? You are looking at it from your own standpoint. You have a different situation than lots of kids who start on drugs.

Bill: I had a good family situation so that wasn't it. Lots of kids don't have a good family situation and they start using drugs. Up until after high school I had never experienced really bad things that I couldn't cope with. I accepted everything as normal. Things were easy for me and then when I started college, I started having emotional problems I had never had before. When I first smoked marijuana, it wasn't because of any problem, it was that I was with a crowd and they were smoking so I just kind of did it. I didn't think it was a terrible wrong and I wasn't afraid. I couldn't see any reason not to.

Betty: He was saying when you take drugs, you are at a low point in your life — you come down from a normal or high to a low.

Joe: Well, I started drugs a little younger than Bill, he only started recently. I will only be 15 this Friday and I was addicted to drugs when I was 13½. I started when I was about 12 or 11. Drugs, themselves, have never been my big problem. Everyone is yelling how it will hurt our parents. How can it hurt them if they don't find out? Will it hurt your parents that much when they do find out? Some parents think "why did my son or my daughter start doing this — where did I go wrong"? We shouldn't worry about that. My parents were not the cause of my taking drugs. My Dad has always been pretty good to me. Whenever I needed anything, he got it for me. Just recently I got away from that. I am making my own money and buying my own clothes. The clothes I have on today are pretty shabby for the simple reason that today I have to go home and pull the transmission. I don't want to wear another pair of clothes and just ruin them with grease and oil.

Yes, I like the clothes I have on — they aren't the best but they are kind of comfortable. No offense to you people — all of you

have on suits and I'm sure you don't enjoy that tie around your
neck cutting off your circulation. Suits and ties aren't supposed to
be that comfortable; they are supposed to make you look richy
and all that stuff. They are absolutely useless when you get right
down to it. I can't see where a pair of slacks and a tie and a sport
jacket are the thing to wear to pull a transmission out of a car! It's
like yelling about something as useless as your parents. Parents ,
have nothing to do with most kids taking drugs. Most kids you
read about in the papers today are out of their homes so their
parents have nothing to do with it. It's got now to where 5th and
6th graders are turned on with dope. I know because I started
when I was in the 6th grade. Soon it will be kindergarten kids. I
started smoking dope before I started smoking cigarettes. The
reason I picked up a cigarette is because a doctor just recently said
I might as well keep on smoking for a while. I smoke 2½ packs a
day because we are allowed to smoke at school, its a privilege. It's
not a set thing, but a privilege. If we put our butts out on the floor
we lose our privilege.

We were talking about depression causing a person to want to
take drugs. Depression wasn't the reason I took drugs all the time.
In fact, when I felt good, I thought that was a good time to take
drugs. I would feel that much better if I was stoned. Anything I
did I thought this would really be cool if I were stoned, like going
swimming. I wanted to be doing everything stoned to see what it
was like.

People think we take drugs when we are depressed. When I
became addicted, I was never depressed. I never even realized I was
addicted, until a month before I got busted, and then I had to try
to get busted, one way or another because I knew I was hooked. I
was leaving bags of grass laying around the house — that didn't get
me busted. I was leaving seeds in my coat, I was going to school
smelling like dope, I was going to school ripped — nothing
happened. I didn't get busted. Then, I realized they weren't going
to get me this way so I started back being sneaky and they
outright got me. I mean, it took them five minutes when I started
coming to school and tried to act normal, started doing grade A
work and they riddled me right over — they knew I was taking
dope. They wanted to get me right out. They hauled me out of

school, made me roll up my sleeves, went over my house with a search warrant and made me clean my bedroom out in half an hour.

I got hooked on drugs accidentally. I did the same thing you were doing; I was trying everything stoned, only it didn't work out for me. One morning I woke up and I had to be stoned before I could roll over and shut off the alarm, I had to be stoned before I could get out of bed, I had to have a joint before I could get up.

Drugs aren't the big thing in most people's lives. There are other things that make them take drugs besides their parents and home life, there are other pressures put on them. I am talking about school, that teacher, she has 30 students and she will one day take the time to finger you right out of that classroom. When I was in 7th grade, right when I started using drugs smashingly heavy, that teacher needled me into cussing her out, she wanted me to do it, she wanted me out of that class. I really let her have it too, she left that room in tears saying she was going to the principal's office. That school really got me down because it was plastic, and all the schools I went to until just recently were plastic. The teachers all try to be so nice and kind and friendly, but it doesn't work that way. They put on an awfully big front, they hide everything from you. In the school I am going to now, if the teachers want to smoke a cigarette in front of the class they do it, if they want to cuss, they do it. Everybody is really himself, they are good teachers and you really learn something from them.

Mary: I feel that reality is both good and bad and you have to be able to accept both issues objectively and be able to digest them without hurting the personality. I don't feel that I would ever try drugs because I am not depressed or I don't see evil, and I feel that I can handle my problems enough so that I can continue living the way I am now and still be happy.

Tom: Maybe the people who take drugs have a few hang-ups, but so do we and I feel that I can be happy without chemicals, and that is the main thing.

Sue: I can see beauty in things without drugs, and I am happy.

It's pleasant to report that all four drug using teens here

stopped taking drugs, and are doing well.

The non-drug using teens are now fitting well into their group adult states, either attending college, working, or married.

This first session was followed by other sessions, which finally worked into presenting the "dialogue team" to various groups.

For instance, at the Western Institute of Drug Studies, the dialogue panel presented their dialogue to 400 attending the Institute.

Later in the fall, the panel, which was shifted somewhat in its members, presented a dialogue before all the principals and vice-principals of the State of Oregon.

Chapter VIII

SUMMARY, DISCUSSION, AND SUGGESTIONS

THIS final chapter is a summation based on the data provided by 345 high school teen-agers, some of whom (180) had not used drugs, some of whom had used and had not stopped using drugs (80), and some of whom had used drugs, but have stopped using drugs (85).

The data will be summarized into headings, from which reflections on the data will be made, as well as suggestions for prevention and treatment of teen-aged drug abuse. Several hints on therapy will be included.

The data gathering method employed in this study utilized questionnaries. It is my impression that the questionnaire in this study has been an effective instrument. The internal evidence indicated from the responses of the respondents, some of which have been reported in previous chapters, indicated that they were ready to reveal and frankly share their thoughts and feelings.

PREVENTIVE ASPECTS AND
THEORETICAL CONSIDERATIONS

I. Teen-agers who do not use drugs stress the following as preventive factors:
  1. Fear.
  2. No need.
  3. Modeling of drug-using peers.
  4. Will power (ego strength, determination, etc.)
  5. Meaningful experience without the use of drugs.

Maslow (1968) quotes from a study of Dove in which it was found that even among chickens, some are "good choosers," that is, they chose a diet which was good for them, and as a result became "... more dominant than poor choosers." Maslow utilized

Dove's data, to infer that some individuals choose forms of "slow suicide." Among those who choose "slow suicide," resulting from bad choice, are drug abusers.

Stated positively, for our non-drug abusing teen-agers, it can be inferred that they are good choosers, hopefully, not only in the matter of drugs, but in other areas of life.

    II. In all three groups (drug users, non-drug users, and former drug users) the word "nothing" appeared among their responses.

        1. Thirty-six per cent of the non-drug using respondents replied to the question, "What would happen, do you think that would cause you to start taking drugs?", with, "nothing," and then gave a reason.

        2. Thirty-two per cent of drug-using teens, replied to the question, "As you think about it, what would you speculate that might help you to get off drugs?," with, "nothing," and then followed with a reason.

        3. Thirty-six per cent of former drug using teens replied to the question, "What would happen to have you start taking drugs again?," with, "nothing," and then gave a reason.

These data suggest that the teen-ager's "life-as-lived" is not a whim, nor is he or she a victim of this or that, but rather the teen-ager plays a crucial and determining part in his or her "lived-life."

An "I don't care" attitude is a choice, and often clung to with purpose, even with an aggressive determination, in spite of help offered.

This raises a critical question: How can a person become "a good chooser"? What methods are available to assist him to turn from being a "bad chooser" to a "good chooser?"

An orientating point of view might be supplied by Farber (1968) whose basic notions concerning will were presented in Chapter II. Farber maintains that there are two types of will, one is a general order of the will and the other type of will helps the person toward a particular or more selected goal. Applying this conception to the present concern, it would appear that if a teen-ager has merely used drugs without really changing his life-style or major goals (education, etc.), it implies that his "basic thinking patterns" are still present. It would be easier for him to decide to stop using drugs, to "get back," or to "hurry-along" toward his original goal, his life direction. Whereas, if a teen-ager has basically changed his life's direction and as a consequence his basic "philosophical-operational" self made the decision to stop using drugs (and to stay stopped), it will not only be more difficult but will encompass more, since his "life direction" must also be altered.

Data can be abstracted which support these assumptions. One girl respondent wrote that in order for her to stop using drugs, she would have "... to get back to my original state of happiness."

Another respondent wrote, "Nothing. I'm satisfied," would induce her to use drugs; and finally, a third respondent was "fence-riding," at times wanting drugs, at times not wanting drugs.

Utilization of these findings can be potentially helpful in working with teens. Thus, helping a teen-ager in the first few months of drug use, can be easier, before a change in "life style" sets in, which confirms the use of drugs, reinforced by peers, etc. Some interesting research findings appear to be appropriate at this point.

Hekimian and Gershan (1968) concluded from their work that,

> ... emotionally disturbed, but younger groups, tended to use marihuana, amphetamines, and hallucinogens. Fifty per-cent of this group was considered schizophrenic before taking drugs and 37% required state hospitalization. Thus, protracted psychotic states thought to be due to drug injections may be due to pre-existing mental disturbances.

Other research findings tend to support the above. Baumann (1970), found in comparing 100 LSD users with non-users, " ... a much higher incidence of psychopathology among LSD users than non-users, with conduct disturbance and psychosis being the most frequent profile diagnosis."

It would seem to follow, that some youthful drug users are incapable of being "good choosers," that the sicker the person (the more psychopathic), the poorer the prospects are for recovery, yet, surprisingly, this does not follow. Baumann found that hypnosis was more successful with LSD users than marijuana users. The individual who combines "good choice" and determination (will power or ego strength), coupled with some "pain" (it begins to hurt) has a fairly good chance to get off drugs.

    III. One of the major findings of the present study relates to the concept of experience. Since this is such a key concept, I intend to interweave the findings with bits of theory, other findings, and clinical assessments so the reader can readily see the application.

Several authors deal with special or different kinds of experience. A few of these materials will briefly be touched upon at this point.

Schachtel (1959) devotes a chapter entitled, "Perception as Creative Experience," reaching the conclusion that an open, fresh, spontaneous encounter with reality produces a creative experience, which in turn is a source of personal growth and, at times, even an inspiration.

Arieti (1967) attempts to treat religious and mystical experience without delineating the basic term experience.

Erickson (1964) differentiates between actuality and reality. In the former condition, a person participates in the world without defenses, while in the latter condition, the participation is a "phenomenal experience," in which an individual perceives the world without distortion. In other words, Erickson is differentiating between a perceived and an actual relationship to the world, and, therefore, different ways of experiencing the world. The mind may, even under hypnosis, be offered an imagined experience which, to all intent and purposes, allows a person in the nonhypnotic state to call upon the imagined experience as if it was an actual event (Giammateo, 1970).

Maslow (1962) presents a discussion on experience and maintains that there is a difference between B, cognition (non-self-centered) and D, cognition (deficiency needs of the individual). The central thrust of Maslow's work referred to here is his efforts to describe, delineate, and explore peak experiences. The interested reader should consult Maslow's book for details.

Keen (1969) states that there are two extreme manners of experiencing the world, the way of Apollo (which is all work) and the way of Dionysius (which is all play) and suggests that a healthy balance of these two is the ideal way to experience one's self and the world.

Suzuki (1960) explains the difference between East and West approaches to reality in the following manner. First, he quotes from a poem by Basho (a Japanese poet):

> When I look carefully
> I see the nazuna blooming
> By the hedge!

A portion of a poem by Tennyson:

> Flower in the crannied wall,
> I pluck you out of the crannies;
> Hold you here, root and all, in my hand.

Then, Suzuki makes the comment,

> The Zen approach is to enter right into the object itself and see it, as it were, from the inside. To know the flower is to become the flower, to be the flower, to bloom as the flower, and to enjoy the sunlight as well as the rainfall.

This, according to Suzuki, is the creative way of knowing or of experiencing.

In a book edited by Tart (1969) an anonymous author contributes a chapter: "The Effect of Marijuana on Consciousness." In this chapter, it is asserted that there are two ways to react to sensory effects:

1. Pure awareness, ". . . is experiencing without associations to what is there."
2. Conscious awareness, ". . . is connected to meanings, plans, functions, decisions, and possible actions."

In the remainder of the chapter, the anonymous author attempts to indicate how marijuana assists its user to experience with "pure awareness" or "enhancement of the immediate experience." Gendlin (1964) tries to describe the steps of client (or patient) undergoes during the process of experiencing. Essentially, for Gendlin, experience is an association (that is, an interaction) between feelings and words (or events, symbols). Gendlin insists that his definition of experience differs from insight, stressing that insight follows an experience.

In my opinion, the concept of *experience* is best explained by Kelly (1955). Kelly treats at length, and in depth, this concept,

saying that experience is, "... made up of the successive con-
struing of events." It is carefully noted by Kelly that, "... it is
learning which constitutes experience," and he suggests humor-
ously and sharply that a person can have the same experience over
and over without expanding one's vision or learning. On a clinical
level, one young, female patient declared, "I got bored, it was like
seeing the same circus over and over," and she stopped using LSD
after two-hundred "trips."

Utilizing Kelly's definition of experience, it would be my
impression that the use of heroin is not an experience, it is simply
a "habit," a dream-like state without dreams. At best, it is a
"ritualized" experience.

Kelly further suggests that a person might "know" many things
which are not true, hence, an individual can have "a variety of
experiences," but his "constructions will be invalid, if his personal
constructs continue to mislead him."

Closely associated with the concept of experience, is that of
altered states of consciousness. At this juncture, a brief presentation on this topic will be given, followed by an effort to "tie-in"
experience and altered state of consciousness with drug abuse.

Martin (1969) in his monumental study of the three religions,
(Christianity, Judaism, and Islam) insists that a change of
consciousness (altered state of awareness) was a crucial and critical
factor (always present) when prophets received a message from
God (Yahweh or Allah). This religious experience is profound and
deep, "beside it," Martin holds, "The exoticism of a psychedelic
trip is but foolish double-talk and a dangerous pathology . . ."

The founder of Alcoholics Anonymous, Bill Wison, as reported
in *Time* magazine (Feb. 8, 1971) prayed for help when hospitalized. "Suddenly," he claimed, "the room lit up with a great white
light. I was caught into an ecstacy which has no words to
describe." For the remainder of his life, Bill Wison had a mission
to fulfill.

The point can be readily grasped is that not every subjective
experience, every altered state of consciousness, is accurate or
"true." I know, for example, many schizophrenic patients who
claim a variety of ungrounded false "messages," and so does every
professional person dealing with schizophrenic persons. History

books are filled with "false prophets," some whose zeal for the messages devastated thousands upon thousands of lives. Hitler affords a convenient example.

Are there any criterion on which standards of evaluation can rest, so as to ascertain a "true" from a "false" "message" or "experience"? Ludwig and associates (1970) note, "Associated with the altered state of consciousness and profound nature of the experience is another important feature; as the patient emerges from this state, he tends to feel a sense of rebirth, rejuvenation, or renaissance. Now that he has undergone this "ordeal," he senses that something profound and unique has happened to him. The experience tends to be viewed subjectively as a new starting point or foundation in his life or a springboard for further action." What is the association between drug experience and the effect on the individual's life? Ludwig and associates write, "Despite the general assumption that the profound emotional and subjective experience associated with psychedelic drugs must affect a person's attitude and belief system, supposedly for the better, there is currently no evidence to support this contention. In fact, knowledge of human nature dictates that people, especially those who are mentally ill, are more apt to interpret their experiences to fit their needs and beliefs than to change their view to fit their experience."

The same type of conclusion was reached by Pahnke and Richards (1966), namely, that although in their experiment, seminary students who were given psilocybin as compared to seminary students given nicotine acid (a vitamin that causes warm and tingling to the skin), the former experiences were a "deeper or better" reaction to Good Friday services, although it did not mean that their future lives would be better or more productive than those who had the lesser experiences.

On a clinical level one of my patients, a 19-year-old male remarked, "Although I had a lot of insights, I couldn't put any of them to use. I just couldn't get going . . ." He stopped using drugs, two years ago, and is now gainfully occupied, and doing an excellent job, helping youthful drug abusers to find a meaningful existence without the use of drugs. Here then, is an instance in which insights achieved under an altered state of consciousness, although subjectively an excellent experience, were fruitless in changing his behavior. The "real" insight was to get off drugs. Another example is that of a 20-year-old male while on an LSD trip, he had "a religious conversion," and saw that his drug behavior was futile, stopped using drugs, came to the clinic, struggled with some deep, emotional conflicts, and today (1½ years later) appears to be happily married, drug free and employed. Here is an example of a "fruitful" experience, utilized to change his life.

Gendlin (1964) has insisted that certain conditions such as hypnosis, dreams, CO_2, LSD, and stimulus deprivation, hinders or "greatly curtails" the manner of experiencing. I would say, not always as noted in the above patient's quotation. One of the key factors is the stopping of LSD. In other words, a few (perhaps some) who have used LSD once, or a few times, have benefitted — they gained an insight, stopped using drugs, and put the insight "to work."

In both instances, and I would assume this to be a common factor, (I know it is so with other individuals) there was no longer a use of psychedelics, in fact, no drugs, including marijuana. Referring to the study by Hekimiam and Gershon (1968) use of drugs can trigger a psychiatric break, in potentially prone individuals. But, what about those who are not psychotic prone or sociopathically oriented, does the use of drugs stimulate the individual to greater "heights" and greater "depths"?

Wilson (1969) presents an insightful reflection when he says, "I do not believe there is any useful short-cut to mystical experience, either psychedelic drugs or so-called yoga disciplines. I am not denying that there are both means of achieving states of "intensity consciousness," any more than I would deny that you can "play" a Beethoven sonata by putting on a gramophone record or working the pedals of a player-piano. But if you wanted to learn to play the Beethoven sonata in the real sense of the word, you would have to start at the beginning, doing scales, and learning to sight-read music. Where mystical experience is concerned, we have the equivalent of "scales," i.e. practical exercises in yoga disciplines. But what we most emphatically do not have is the equivalent of a musical scale, the detailed objective knowledge of what goes on in states of "intensity consciousness." In my own investigation, I have preferred the careful, plodding attempt to create a kind of mental "musical notation" to the mystical vagaries of some writers on cosmic consciousness."

Giammatteo (1970) adds to the present discussion when he mentions that at a "structure level" an individual feels he must control his environment, and when this fails, he will escape to fantasy, and ". . . fantasy becomes part of his structuring." Applied to our present study, the teen-ager who feels "up-tight," weak, helpless, or angry, but unable to control the *establishment,* resorts to fantasy (drug use) and in this manner will attempt to structure (control) his environment. Frequently, he now mobilizes numbers of people (parents, siblings, peers, teachers, and professional individuals) to help him, whereas, previously he was, for all practical purposes, ignored or ineffective. He was not structuring reality, now he is structuring.

The critical factor, as I see it, is not just having "an experience," (it can be useless, erroneous, harmful, psychotic, etc.) but rather, the experience should be constructive, valuable, expanding, authentic, enjoyable, enabling, etc.

If the teen-ager finds experience (happiness, meaning, involvement, purpose, joy, etc.) in his life without the use of drugs, chances are he will not use drugs. The data of the present research suggest that numerous non-drug using teen-agers reported no need for drugs; they were happy and having "an experience" of a type which might be termed "in-depth," or "growth" or "involvement," etc. Perhaps, somewhat similar to Charlie Brown, flying a kite can be an emotional experience for them. They have the ability to enhance and to savor many of the natural, routine events of life, relationships, study, religion, family, nature, etc.

In my other works (1967, 1970) and in the 1971 work, research on adolescents revealed their ability to describe significant experiences. For example, a teen-age boy stated, "I felt wild and excited, as I came in with the waves, I let out screams and rebel yells of wild joy," describing his first surfboard ride.

A teen-age girl described a vacation experience in the following manner, "I enjoy myself more at this time than any other. Being near the lake and the sand dunes gives me a wonderful feeling, it's stimulating to get up in the cool, crisp morning and splash creek water on my face. The days seem long and are packed with fun and exciting events."

Another teen-aged girl (1971) reflected, "Probably the happiest event as such, was more of an *experience*. I go to the beach (Pacific Ocean) very frequently. Last summer while living down at the coast, being on the beach was an every day thing. One day I was walking alone and suddenly had an elevated, fantastic feeling. For the first time, I could see all things, sand, water, rocks, gulls and people, fitting together in a total continuity. I felt I was apart from everything and everyone and I was looking in on the whole scene around me, yet I felt a definite oneness with all around me, a feeling that I really "fit" into a place on the universe." Apparently this teen-age girl could take a "natural trip," or have "an experience" without resorting to the use of drugs.

Other teen-agers have been able to capture the "aftermath" of an involvement and "turn" it into an experience. For example, a teen-age girl wrote, "The last night of a play called *Company of Wayward Saints* had been a strain; I had gone without much sleep for the previous month. It was a terribly exhilarating *experience* to have it done, to be able to relax and know that it was well done. It was our best night, and really quite a spiritually uplifting play. It made one believe in human nature."

An adolescent boy remarked, "In August, our Lutheran League made a 29 mile trip hike over the Cascade Range to Holden Village. There were thirteen of us. In the nine days, all communication barriers went down. Everyone shared everything with the others. Everyone was on equal ground with everyone else. Truly even the most obvious differences were covered by the trail dirt (even sexes). We carried each other's load, both physically and mentally." These, and numerous hundreds of quotes from teen-agers clearly indicate their ability to have healthy, enabling, expanding, and enriching experiences.

If experience of this sort is absent from the "lived-life" of the teen-ager, "magic means" (drugs) will be sought and used. However, some teen-agers become lost in the "magic means" and seemingly are satisfied in this "dream-life" of drugs.

I've termed this kind of experience an "Alice-in-acid-land" episode, and see it similar to an "affair" with drugs, not as an expanding, authentic commitment to the self, nor to another, nor to the community.

As I review the present data and the works of other authors, the following kinds or types of experiences suggest themselves:

1. A routine experience: This category tends to imply that the "life" or "zest" has gone out of the performance of the act. This includes religious rituals, work, sexual intercourse, a beautiful sunset, study, dancing, whatever it is, the "inside-stuff," is "lost."

2. An escape experience: This type of activity is used as an avoidance technique, for instance, alcohol for the alcoholic, drugs for the drug user.

3. An "enabling" or "enriching" experience: With this type of experience the individual can "build on," have deeper inter-personal relations, or enlarge his own "inner-horizon" or his own "inner-space," to plume hidden vistas, in himself, in others, and in the environment, on which he can become wiser, more philosophical, more socially minded, more thoughtful, and more responsible. For instance, after one discussion panel, composed of drug using and non-drug using teens, given at a high school, with an apparently excellent impact, the following summary appeared on the bulletin board.

BULLETIN BOARD

Take Time to Think

1. Plan for a future.
2. Develop Self-control.
3. Understand parent problems.
4. Make own decisions — weigh advice.
5. Control your environment — do not let your environment control you.
6. Learn to handle your problems appropriately.
7. Tolerate others who have troubles.
8. Learn to talk with people young and old.

HAVE FAITH IN SOMETHING

In another work (1971) I have indicated those factors which form the foundation for a happy person, that work can be consulted by the interested reader.

Junior high school is the danger time for the initial use of drugs for many young students. Preventive measures, didactic, group discussion, modeling of drug users, and the like, should be employed at this period in the youngster's life. The present findings disagree with Blachley's (1969) contention that education is all but useless. Some students (and we are interested in *all* students) do benefit from didactic courses on the dangers of drug abuse.

One of the principals in the Portland area related that, in his opinion, drug use was not increasing, perhaps even waning, assigned drug education as the helpful effective agent.

Family discussions are a means which parents can use to help their children, as well as bring the family closer; engaging in an open dialogue is one measure against drug use.

Our family engages in weekly, family discussions on a variety of topics. Recently drugs were the topic. The topic was introduced by Maureen (11 years of age) who informed us that her school was to study drugs the coming week. The discussion got quickly "air borne"; I jotted the following.

Tim (10 years of age) said, "Any drug could be harmful, if used incorrectly."

Mrs. Scott (Kathy) asked, "Does Molly (7 years of age) know what a drug is?"

Tim: "Like it said in the *Oregonian,* maybe a kid can't grasp what a drug is, but if he eats or drinks too much, he gets sick. He can understand that!"

Mrs. Scott: "What's a drug, Molly? Have you ever taken one?"

Molly: "I don't know."

Mrs. Scott: "Have you taken an aspirin?"

Molly: "Yes, and I take allergy pills. If I take two, okay, if I take 10 pills, I could kill myself."

Tim: "How do you know that?"

Molly: "I was listening to Mommy. Any pill, if I took too much can get me sick."

Kathleen (16 years of age): "So, Molly, you can see, it's easier for you to understand about being sick, than drugs."

Molly: "Yea, and when you have a baby around, you should keep pills up high."

Maureen "How'd you know that?"

Molly: "On T.V. commercials."

Mrs. Scott: "Tim, what would you do if someone, one of your friends, or one of the kids at school, asked you to take drugs?"

Tim: "I'd beat him up."

Mike (15 years of age): "Come on, none of that nonsense. What would you do?"

Tim: "I'd just, oh, it depends on what they'd call me; I'd say, it's too bad for you, taking the drugs."

Mrs. Scott: "When you look around your room, do you think some of the students might be using drugs?"

Kathleen: "I know some sweet kids who use drugs."

Mike: "I think you can walk into a class and spot the ones who don't care about anything, they most often use drugs."

Mrs. Scott: "If someone asked you to take drugs, would you?"

Maureen: "I'd say, forget it."

Dr. Scott: "What if you're invited to a party and most of the kids are smoking marijuana?"

Marueen: "I'd leave."

Mike: "Would you report them?"

Maureen: "I don't know. If I liked them, I wouldn't. Is it against the law not to report them?"

Mrs. Scott: "No, unless you were asked; also, if you were at a party where drugs were being used, you're guilty."

Kathleen: "Mike, what if someone asked you to take drugs?"

Mike: "Once a guy kinda did, he said, 'You can have some,' and I said, It's not that important. If you say it's really dumb, they only try harder; most drug users are in cliques, and if you pick on one, they all gang up on you."

Mrs. Scott: "Kathleen, what if someone asked you to take drugs?"

Kathleen: "I'd stop and think and remember. Under pressure, you can't just jump and say no. I've been asked. I said I'm happy the way I am."

The family proceeded with the discussion. From a very subjective point of view, I felt it was an excellent dialogue, one which has also borne fruit. Giammatteo suggests that each child and adult in the family accept two full minutes per week of having *good* things pointed out about them. Giammatteo notes it is difficult at first for family members to point out good because most of their practice in giving feedback is around negative concerns. At first, the pointing out of good focuses in on clothing, hair style, etc. But within a week or two the weekly sessions end up pointing out good behaviors that are not superficial. Giammatteo implies that family members have difficulty accepting positive feedback as well as with giving it. Thus this weekly pointing out of good causes the focus of attention on *observing* good things, on the one hand, and on *doing* good thing, on the other.

The majority of teen-aged drug users of the present sample utilize a variety (3 or more) of drugs. Seemingly only a minority maintain on marijuana.

The WHO Technical Report (1967) states,

> Another phenomenon has been observed recently in the U.S.A., namely, the use of sequence of quite different drugs, for example, the use by a group of adolescents first of barbiturates for a limited period, then alcohol for a few days, followed by heroin, amphetamines, marijuana, LSD, and so on.

Former drug users differ with regard to the question concerning their use of drugs. Some state they wish they had not used drugs because of the problems, the memories, etc. Others reported that they had learned a valuable lesson, but had no wish to "re-learn" it.

Non-drug using teens often reject their drug using peers, and vice versa.

The launching of panel discussions using both drug abusing and non-drug using teens, was based on the above finding. The utilization of this modality, for drug education, drug prevention, and drug treatment has vast potential.

Over two years ago, I moderated a panel discussion between four drug abusing and four non-drug using teen-agers before 500 principals and vice-principals from the State of Oregon. This program was so well received I was literally "hounded" by the principals to put on such a program for their student bodies and for their P.T.A. groups. It was such an overwhelming task, in addition to my other duties, I could not do it. At this point, Mr. Paulus was added to the clinic staff in order to help. His chapter

(Chapter VI), which relates his activities with groups of students and parents, affords ample evidence to the potential in this kind of program. The reader can recall some of the comments recorded in Chapter VII, between the drug users and non-drug using teens.

Numerous references to the continual benefit of this kind of dialogue could be reported. I want to state that this particular type of dialogue is an effective preventive element for non-drug using teens and a treatment modality for drug using teen-agers.

My oldest daughter, Kathleen, has participated on some of the panel discussions and has found it to be a personally rewarding experience.

Those teen-agers who have stopped using drugs, usually do not endorse the use of drugs for their peers.

Conflict, in the teen lingo "up-tight," is not harmful, nor is it to be avoided at all costs. Conflict is one means to develop "psychological muscles." Drug abuse contributes to "psychological flabbiness."

I would like to indulge myself in a bit of fantasy, applying a fairy tale to the present issue — conflict.

Pinocchio is a fairy tale, familiar, I would suppose, to everyone. The reader will recall Mr. Gippetto's astonishment to find his carved puppet alive, "The mouth was not even completed when it began to laugh and deride him." A long series of events ensue in which the parent (Mr. Gippetto) had absolutely no influence over his son, Pinocchio, nor did the conscience, in the form of the talking cricket. In desperation, the ineffective conscience announces, "But if you do not wish to go to school, why not at least learn a trade, if only to enable you to earn honestly a piece of bread?"

Pinocchio reported that he had no interest either in school or in work, but wished, ". . . to lead a vagabond life from morning to night."

"As a rule," said the talking cricket, "all those who follow that trade end always either in a hospital or in prison."

The remaining adventures of Pinocchio tell a tale of mischief, of continual failure, even the good fairy (therapists, friends, well wishers) could not help, until Pinocchio faced his failures.

Perhaps, by a stretch of the imagination, Pinocchio is typical of many teen-agers, unwilling to face conflict, utilizing many means of escape, drug use being but one avenue of avoidance.

Quotations from numerous respondents rather clearly indicate this element. For instance, recall the quote (Chap. IV) of a 17-year-old girl, "Guilt. I was seeing my friends get hung up on drugs; seeing the ones I'd started on drugs get busted. I was getting so I couldn't take the crashing, so I'd get ripped again. It was costing too much. I was lying to myself. I realize it was only an escape."

As long as drug using teen-agers receive what is judged to be a benefit (an experience, a "trip," "kicks," etc.) from their use of drugs, and the price is not too high (pain, fear, sickness, etc.), they will continue to use drugs.

Respondents who stopped using drugs, in the majority of instances, related that "internal-reasons" (fear, emotional problems, bummers, no pay-off) rather than "external reasons" (family, friends, etc.) were the generating motives for stopping the use of drugs.

Self-survival reasons are the most effective in the changing of behavior. Altruism, loyalty, and faithfulness appear to be second rate motives, once an individual becomes dependent on some activity or substance, whether it is alcohol, drugs, smoking, etc. If their inner motives were operative, the individual would not have become dependent in the first instance.

Once off drugs, former users replied that fear continued as a motive, but other factors were important. A continual determination (will power) was especially essential for teen-aged boys, whereas, the teen-aged girls reported friends were important reasons for remaining off drugs.

Drug use most likely starts out to solve some kind of particular problem (to belong to a group), or goal (to find "kicks"), hence, a search for something more than mere escape. In other words, it is a yearning for "meaning," or to have an "experience," but if drug use continues, it then becomes a "life style," similar to an alcoholic.

IV. Community Response to Drug Use:

MacAndrew and Edgerton (1969) found in their research that, "people quickly learn to take advantage and to know the limits.

They write, "We would now note that these three peoples had something else in common as well, in all three instances, when the drunken transgressions in question occurred, they were without serious consequences for the transgressions." In other words, how one acts, and what one does in a society, when drunk, is often a learned behavior, so also, with drug use. If drug users are not held responsible for their behavior, they will use this as "time out" (in the terms of MacAndrew and Edgerton), so it does not count.

Both society and the individual share in a joint responsibility:

1. Society must provide an arena of opportunity for its citizens.
2. Society's laws must be equitable and reasonable.
3. Each citizen must assume personal responsibility for his choices and for his actions.

V. Prevention:

This section concerns itself with family exercises which have been helpful, for our family, and hopefully, will be for other families.

The "exercises" are geared to help each member of the family, and the family as a whole, to grow in the art of experiencing the self and the other, and as a result to live more fully and to appreciate each other more deeply.

1. All the members of the family lie down in a circle (feet forward) on the floor, with eyes closed. The family members take turns in using one of the five senses. For instance, all are asked "to hear something beautiful," then all take turns relating what he heard. Secondly, all are asked to "see something beautiful" and then all take turns relating what was seen. This same kind of exercise continues with the other three senses.

   After all five senses are "exercised," a discussion is started by "which sense do you most like (or appreciate)?" It must be made clear that this question does not imply that you would lose any sense, rather (keeping all five senses) which one you "like" the best. Usually, family members differ as to their choice and a discussion ensues.

2. At the next session, a discussion revolved around, "How can I learn to appreciate another one of my senses?" This goal is

reached by a shared family exercise, for instance, all
listening to music, or all smelling flowers in the yard, or the
odors from the kitchen (fresh bread, etc.) or by touching
each other, etc.

3. Another exercise typically enjoyed by all family members is
the following: "Act out an emotion," and the rest of the
family members guess which emotion it is.

4. Another family exercise is to plan on having a new
experience of a deepening emotional experience, in the
coming week and express it the next week.

5. Poems can be read and members of the family asked to
evaluate and compare the meaning, the beauty and the
emotion. For example, the poems quoted by Suzuki (earlier
in the book) were read and all the family members were
asked to react to them, to compare them. This was followed
by a discussion gleaned from this project.

6. Our family has found that reading for a few minutes at the
supper table is an enjoyable event. Some of the family
favorites have been, *Charlotte's Webb* by E. B. White and
The Little Prince by DeSaint-Exupery.

These and other exercises have been avenues for closeness, experiencing, and happiness for our family. I am
certain the reader can, with a little imagination, add
"favorites" for his family.

Doing therapy with drug using teen-agers, I have found
that when not under the influence of drugs, they find it
difficult to express their feelings or to employ their
imagination.

It is hoped that family exercises will be an avenue of
help for them, and a means of preventive help for
youngsters.

VI. A Look to the Future:

I feel that drug use will begin to decline. The drug user will
learn that drugs is neither a panacea nor a cure, either for his
personal problems (or desires) nor for society's. Non-drug users
will be more and more impressed by the ill-effects, so aptly
modeled by drug users.

As reports reach the literature concerning the deleterious

effects of drug use, coupled with a "public-push," drug use will diminish. By this, I mean, the use of drugs for the so-called normal or average teen-ager and youth.

For the seriously maladjusted and malcontent, use of narcotics (hard drugs) will continue, although some in-roads will be made by new rehabilitation practices for some individuals.

The country will see attempts of various factions advocating particular life styles, Synanon, communes, counter-culture, and alternate culture groups.

It is my thought that the more militant groups will survive; the others will become disillusioned and fractionate; many others will become future social hurdles.

VII. Conclusion:

I want to conclude this book with quotes from two teen-agers who seem to summarize in an accurate and authentic manner, the tasks, struggles, and solutions for all teen-agers.

Why I Don't Need Drugs

Mike (15 years old)

The reason why I don't use drugs is best summarized in one word, responsibility; to my town or community, to my friends, to my family, but most important, the valued responsibility to myself.

My town, my friends, and my family have done a lot for me in fifteen years. If I were to take drugs, it would be like flicking it all in their faces, for the good schools, the treasured memories, and their love. Right now, I couldn't do that. I need what they gave me. I need to do what is expected of me, and this keeps me close to them. Besides, I didn't work hard in the summers (picking berries, cucumbers, working in the potato fields), do my chores, and go to school for nine years, just to blow all that, and much more, for a few pills or shots of dope.

Then, too, the way to drugs is to do it because everyone else does it; or a silly follow-the-leader game of the big fellow takes drugs, so! But, I'm a leader too! A fellow needs to be a leader, to get places today. Just to follow some kid who chooses to blow his responsibilities, would be stupid and in direct opposition to my standards.

I know a number of teen-agers who I think take drugs to become a big shot, and to get praise from some of the kids on drugs. I don't need this kind of thing. It might be okay for others to start taking drugs, but not for me. My friends don't praise me for not taking drugs, though if I did, my *new* friends would.

I have enough attention at home and at school. At home, I'm loved and respected, and cheered on. At school, I get sufficient attention from: (a) playing football (I was the defensive captain), (b) from winning my share on the wrestling team, and (c) from good grades (mostly A's, with an occasional B).

I don't need any more attention from taking drugs and I don't need drugs to do my thing. I say to myself, "I'm doing everything just okay," so I feel comfortable within myself. Yea, I can dish out the attention, if I choose.

My reasons might not be sufficient for other teen-agers to stay off drugs, but they satisfy my needs."

Why I Don't Need Drugs

Kathleen (16 years old)

I do not take drugs simply because I do not feel the need. I can honestly say that my life has been smooth enough and easy enough that I do not need pills and needles for a crutch. Now, don't get me wrong, I'm not saying that everything goes right for me and that I am always happy. This is not so. I am human, I do have rough times. But when things go wrong for me, I can usually sit down and reason things out with myself, or often with my parents. I say usually, because many times I get carried away and scream at everyone in sight. "It's all your fault," which is utterly ridiculous, because it couldn't possibly be *all* their fault and often times it couldn't even be *partly* their fault. Most often, it's all *my* fault.

But even when I have these trying times, I still come through without drugs to pull me through.

Not only this, but I just could not lose everything I have going for me; a wonderful family, beautiful home, good education, close and casual friends, and a beautiful world that has the sun shining constantly (even if it is raining).

I can see all the beauty of the world, birds singing, clear skies, green grass, flowers blooming, sunset and sunrise, snow-capped mountains, and rain, all this with my own eyes, without any crutch at all. It really gives me a self-satisfaction to be able to do this.

And yet, I am not only concerned with what would happen to the present, I am also concerned with my future. I plan on having lots of fun growing up, I plan to make something of the life I was given. I just could not take drugs and make my life worthless. I want to get a good job, I want to raise a family, I want to do all these things without a pill, a needle or a smoke.

I simply do not feel the need, that's why I don't take drugs and don't think I ever will.

BIBLIOGRAPHY

1. Arieti, S.: The Intrapsychic Self. New York, Basic Books, 1967.
2. Baumann, F.: Hypnosis and the adolescent drug abuser. Amer. J. Clin. Hypn., 13:17-21, 1970.
3. Blachly, P.: Seduction as a Conceptual Model in the Drug Dependencies. Presented in part at the 31st annual meeting of the committee on problems of drug dependence. Div. of Med. Sci., Nat. Acad. of Sciences, Nat. Research Council, Palo Alto, Feb., 26, 1969.
4. Blum, R. and Associates: Students and Drugs. San Francisco, Jossey-Bass, 1970, vol. II, p. 370.
5. Carroll, Lewis: Through the Looking Glass. 2nd ed. London, Macmillan & Co., 1866.
6. Cohen, S.: The drug dilemma: A partial solution. In Resource Book for Drug Abuse Education. Chevy Chase, U.S. Dept. of H.E.W. Public Health Service, Oct. 1969, pp. 14-17.
7. Cudrin, J.: Self concepts of prison inmates. J. Relig. Health, 1970, ch. 9, pp. 60-70.
8. Douvan, Elizabeth and Adelson, J.: The Adolescent Experience. New York, John Wiley & Sons, 1966.
9. Erickson, E.: Insight and Responsibility. New York, W. W. Norton, 1964.
10. Eveloff, H.: The LSD syndrome. Calif. Med., 109, 368-373, 1968.
11. Farber, L.: The Ways of the Will. New York, Harper Colophon Books, 1968.
12. Frosch, W.: Chapter II, Patterns of response to self administration of LSD. In Drug Abuse. Eds. Cole, J. and Wittenborn, J. Springfield, Charles C Thomas, 1969.
13. Fromm, E., Suzuki, and deMartine, R.: Zen Buddhism and Psychoanalysis. New York, Harper & Bros., 1960.
14. Fuller, E.: Flight. New York, Random House, 1970.
15. Gendlin, E.: Chapter IV, A theory of personality change. In Personality Change. Eds. Worchel, P. and Byrne, D. New York, John Wiley & Sons, 1964.
16. Giammatteo, M.: The Flow to Separation. Portland, Northwest Regional Educational Laboratory, 1970.
17. Giammatteo, M.: Structuring, Communicating and Explaining Lines of Behavior — Prototype Level Project. Portland, Northwest Regional Educational Laboratory, 1969.
18. Garodetzky, C.: Marihuana, LSD and amphetamines. In Drug Dependence. Chevy Chase, National Institute of Mental Health, 5:18-23, 1970.
19. Gould, R.: Chapter XII, The mariginally asocial personality: The

beatnik-hippie alienation. In The World Biennial of Psychiatry and Psychotherapy. Ed. S. Arieti, New York, Basic Books, vol. I, 1971, p. 277.

20. Hekimian, L. and Gershon, S.: Characteristics of drug abusers admitted to a psychiatric hospital. J.A.M.A., 205:125-130, 1968.

21. Hollister, L.: Marihuana in man: Three years later. Science, 172:21-28, 1971.

22. Jones, Mary: Personality correlates and antecedents of drinking patterns in adult males. J. Consult. Clin. Psychol., 32:2-12, 1968.

23. Kelly, G.: The Psychology of Personal Constructs. New York, W. W. Norton, 1955, vol. I.

24. Keen, S.: Apology for Wonder. New York, Harper & Row, 1969.

25. Leary, T.: The politics, ethics and meaning of marihuana. In The Marihuana Papers. Ed. D. Solomon, Signet Books. 3rd printing. New York, New American Library, Inc., 1966.

26. Lennard, H., Epstein, L., Bernstein, A. and Ransom, D.: Mystification and Drug Misuse. San Francisco, Jossey-Bass, 1971, p. 54.

27. Ludwig, A., Levine, J. and Stark, L.: LSD and Alcoholism. Springfield, Charles C Thomas, 1970, p. 59.

28. MacAndrew, C. and Edgerton, R.: Drunken Compartment. Chicago, Aldine, 1969.

29. Martin, M.: The Encounter. New York, Farrar, Straus & Girioux, 1969, p. 8.

30. Maslow, A.: Toward a Psychology of Being. Princeton, D. van Nostrand, 1962.

31. Maslow, A.: Toward a Humanistic Biology (first draft). Menlo Park, W. P. Laughlin Foundation, 1968.

32. Masterson, J., Jr.: The Psychiatric Dilemma of Adolescence. Boston, Little, Brown and Co., 1967.

33. May, R.: Love and Will. New York, W. W. Norton, 1969.

34. Pahnke, W. and Richards, W.: Implications of LSD and Experimental Mysticism. J. Relig. Health, 5:175-208, 1966.

35. Rinzler, C. and Shapiro, D.: Wrist-Cutting and Suicide. J. Mount Sinai Hospital, no. 5, 35:485-488, 1968.

36. Robbins, Lillian; Robbins, E. and Stern, M.: Psychological and environmental factors associated with drug use. In Drug Dependence. National Institute of Mental Health, no. 5, 1-6, 1970.

37. Salisburg, W. and Fertig, Frances: The myth of alienation and teen-age drug use: Coming of age in mass society. In Resource Book for Drug Abuse Education. Public Health Service. Chevy Chase, Supt. of Documents, U.S. Gov't. Printing Office, Oct. 1969.

38. Saslow, G.: Chapter XVII. Where do we go from here? In Drug Abuse: Data and Debate. Ed. P. Blachly. Springfield, Charles C Thomas, 1970.

39. Schachtel, E.: Metamorphosis. New York, Basic Books, 1959.

40. Scott, E.: An Arena for Happiness. Springfield, Charles C Thomas, 1971.

41. Scott, E.: Struggles in an Alcoholic Family. Springfield, Charles C Thomas, 1970.
42. Scott, E.: Chapter XII, Happiness: Some findings between non-drug using and drug using teen-agers. In Drug Abuse: Data and Debate. Ed. P. Blachly. Springfield, Charles C Thomas, 1970.
43. Scott, E.: Happiness: Protocols of teen-agers. Bulletin: Guild of Cathol. Psychol., 14:69-82, 1967.
44. Sherif, M. and Sherif, Carolyn: Problems of Youth. Chicago, Aldine, 1965.
45. Smart, R. and Jones, Dianne: Illicit LSD Users: Their Personality and Psychopathology. J. Abnorm. Psychol., 75:286-292, 1970.
46. Tart, C.: Altered States of Consciousness. New York, John Wiley, 1969.
47. Thomas, W.: Showdown at generation gap. Farm Journal, March, 1971.
48. Wilson, C.: Poetry and Mysticism. San Francisco, City Lights, 1969.
49. W.H.O. (World Health Organization) Technical Report, Series no. 363, Services for the Prevention and Treatment of Alcohol and Other Drugs, Geneva, 1967.

INDEX

A

Acid
nicotine, 109
slang for LSD, 8 *See also* LSD
use of term by "Jane," 70, 71, 72, 78
description of effects of, 71-2
See also Trip
use of term by patient, 11, 54
Acting out, in Masterson study, 50
Activist
new, as one teenage type, 5
reactionary, as one teenage type, 5
Activity
as reason for not taking drugs, 36, 38, 39
as reason for stopping drug use, 54
Actuality, as differentiated from reality, 106
Addiction, physical, 50
to "hard" narcotics, 13
among Civil War soldiers, 14
to opium, 78
to tranquilizers and sedatives, 12
treatment of with methadone, 14-5
unaware of, 100
See also Hooked; Psychological dependence; Psychic dependence
Addictive, work as, 90
Adelson, 38
Adolescent gap
rationale for use of term, 3-6
seen in rejection of drug users by non-drug users, 36
within one person, 6
Adolescents, *See* Teenagers
Age
of drug users worked with by Paulus, 81
getting lower and lower, 100

junior high as critical, 41, 114
in Masterson study, 50
when drug use began, 41, 50, 52, 81, 99, 100, 101
Alcohol, 48
claimed that marijuana is as safe as, 64, 82
clinical case involving, 21
in combination with barbituates, 13
controversy surrounding, 19-20
dependence on, 118
as escape, 113
hangover after use of, 94
historical note on, 19
implications, 21
physical effects of, 19
slang names for, 19
as social drug, 14, 69
as source of danger, 19
as source of enjoyment instead of drugs, 37, 39, 45
use of by teenagers, 18-9
used with other drugs, 116
why used, 19
Alcohol and Drug Treatment and Training Center of Oregon, 81
Alcoholics Anonymous, 108
Alcoholism, 19, 37
Alice in Wonderland, 40
"Alice-in-acid-land" experience, 112
Alienated
hostile, as one teenage type, 5
youth, 64
Alienation, 44
Allah, 108
Allergy pills, 114
American Medical Association, 3, 20
Committee on Alcoholism and Drug Dependence on Marijuana, 17
American Psychological Association, 3
Amphetamines, 10-12, 95

127